OSPREY COMBAT AIRCRAFT • 2

B-26
MARAUDER UNITS
OF THE EIGHTH
AND NINTH AIR FORCES

SERIES EDITOR: TONY HOLMES

OSPREY COMBAT AIRCRAFT • 2

B-26 MARAUDER UNITS
OF THE EIGHTH
AND NINTH AIR FORCES

Jerry Scutts

OSPREY
AEROSPACE

First published in Great Britain in 1997 by Osprey Publishing,
Midland House, West Way, Botley, Oxford OX2 0PH, UK
44-02 23rd St, Suite 219, Long Island City, NY 11101, USA
Email: info@ospreypublishing.com

Osprey Publishing is part of the Osprey Group.

Transferred to digital print on demand 2010

First published 1997
1st impression 1997

Printed and bound in Great Britain.

A CIP catalogue record for this book is available from the British Library

ISBN: 978 1 85532 637 8

Edited by Tony Holmes
Page design by TT Designs, T & B Truscott
Index by Alan Thatcher
Cover Artwork by Iain Wyllie
Aircraft Profiles by Tom Tullis
Figure Artwork by Mike Chappell
Scale Drawings by Mark Styling

Acknowledgements
The author would like to thank everyone who responded to requests for photographs and data for
inclusion in this volume, and in particular Jim Crow, Tim Bivens, Roger Freeman and Ron MacKay.
Due acknowledgement is also given to the following essential works of reference; *Bridge Busters,
The story of the Crusaders, Marauder Men, Silver Streaks, Ninth Air Force Story, To Win the Winter
Sky, Support and Strike!, Rivenhall, JG 26, IV./Jagdgeschwader 3, The Marauder Thunder* and,
most of all, 'RAF's' numerous books on the B-26 and Eighth and Ninth Air Forces.

Editor's note
To make this best-selling series as authoritative as possible, the editor would be extremely
interested in hearing from any individual who may have relevant photographs, documentation or
first-hand experiences relating to the elite pilots, and their aircraft, of the various theatres of war.
Any material used will be fully credited to its original source. Please contact Tony Holmes at
16 Sandilands, Chipstead, Sevenoaks, Kent, TN13 2SP or via email at tony.holmes@zen.co.uk

The Woodland Trust
Osprey Publishing is supporting the Woodland Trust, the UK's leading woodland conservation
charity, by funding the dedication of trees.

www.ospreypublishing.com

Front cover
B-26G-1 43-34181 (code letters Y5-O) *Lak-a-Nookie* leads fellow 459th Bomb Squadron
(BS)/344th Bomb Group (BG) B-26B-50 42- 95967 (Y5-P) *Rosie O'Brady* through typically
flak-speckled European skies in October 1944. The latter bomber remained in service
through to VE-Day, completing over 140 missions whilst flying with the 344th. The first of
these sorties was flown with Lt W D Brady at the controls, hence the aircraft's nickname,
which was retained by subsequent crews assigned to the combat veteran long after its tour-
expired namesake had returned to the USA. Like *Rosie O'Brady*, *Lak-a-Nookie* also survived
the war (*cover painting by Iain Wyllie*).

CONTENTS

Author's Introduction

Of the quartet of light, attack and medium bombers which saw service with the US Army Air Forces (USAAF) in World War 2, none proved to be such a 'political football' as Martin's B-26 Marauder. By trying to replicate the bomber's early low level attack success in the Pacific, USAAF chiefs failed to appreciate that this method of operation was far too risky for either the southern or western European theatres of war – heavy combat losses were the result of such erroneous tactics.

This unexpected turn of events coincided with a spate of training crashes involving the B-26 in the USA, and the two episodes combined to swiftly bring forth official condemnation – fed by ill-informed rumour – that stated that the fast, and innovative, Marauder was essentially a 'pilot killer'. Having endured three Senate hearings that were bent on terminating production of the Martin bomber altogether during its brief front-line career, the Marauder was swiftly retired immediately after World War 2. In the meantime, revised training procedures, new production models and more realistic operational deployment had resulted in the B-26 becoming one of the USAAF's most effective weapons of war.

From being used in what amounted to an 'attack' role in the early stages of the war, things changed for the B-26 when it became a 'medium' bomber per se. In any event, the convenient pre-war categories for twin-engined US aircraft very quickly became blurred under combat conditions so that the North American B-25 Mitchell (medium) also became an outstanding 'strafer' (attack), the Douglas A-20 Havoc (attack) performed well as a bombardier-carrying medium and the Douglas A-26 Invader could handle either role in its stride. The B-26 remained a 'pure' medium for most of its career, however, which meant that it dropped a modest load of bombs in level flight, slogging its way through to the target in close formation. Crews invariably braved murderous flak, inclement weather and fighter attack to perform their job in the Marauder.

Many individual aircraft performed this deadly routine 100 times or more, and one Martin bomber from the Ninth Air Force – the largest user of the B-26 – achieved fame for doing it no less than 202 times. This record of the eight Marauder groups that made up the core of the Ninth's medium bomber force for about 19 crucial months of World War 2 is respectfully, and admiringly, dedicated to all the crews who gave their lives in that endeavour.

A PHOENIX RISING

'You cannot fly up and down this coast in a bomber at 50 feet and survive.'

With these words, contained in a letter to USAAF chief 'Hap' Arnold in late May 1943, Eighth Air Force boss Brig Gen Ira C Eaker effectively cancelled low-level missions by medium bombers from Britain for the immediate future. The reason for this high level communication was the outcome of the second Imjuiden raid by Martin B-26 Marauders on 17 May, which had recorded the loss of ten out of the eleven aircraft despatched on the mission. The sobering results of the dangerous, and ill-advised, repeat raid on the power station on the Dutch coast by the 322nd BG did not appear to bode well for the B-26's future in combat over Europe. Crew morale was severely shaken, while the officers of the parent 3rd Wing of the Eighth Air Force were forced to look again at the whole concept of incorporating tactical medium bombers into a predominantly strategic offensive.

By late 1942 Martin of Baltimore had completed eight models of the Marauder, and was tooling up to commence construction of the improved B-26B-10. All early aircraft had the short 65-ft wingspan and small vertical tail surfaces synonymous with the original prototypes and pre-production airframes, as did the B-26C-5-MO, the first production model built at the new Army-run Martin plant at Omaha, Nebraska.

Numerous camouflage schemes were tried early in World War 2 to break up the outline of aircraft, Marauders, for example, being adorned with blotches of medium green over standard olive drab on upper surfaces in the pattern shown here. Short wing and tail B-26s were both light and exceptionally manoeuvrable, but nowhere near rugged enough for combat in the ETO. A single gun tail position was also considered inadequate, experience showing that at least two .50 cal Brownings were needed to fend off enemy fighters with any level of success (*MAP*)

The bomber made its combat debut with the 22nd BG in the Pacific in early 1942, whilst the first Marauders to engage the Germans in action belonged to the Twelfth Air Force's 319th BG, who flew their initial sorties from Maison Blanche, in Algeria, later that same year on 28 November – the RAF had started flying Marauder Is on operational missions some four months prior to this. In England, the Eighth Air Force's 322nd BG received its first B-26B-2s, B-3s and B-4s in March 1943, and following intense training, flew its first sorties on 14 May.

The latter group's factory-fresh B-4s, with their distinctive 'stepped' tail gun position, were the result of the most recent product improvement programme implemented by Martin following feedback from the frontline. Throughout its brief production life the B-26 was constantly being 'tinkered' with, and one of the major changes embodied on this particular variant was the inclusion of a strengthened nosewheel leg, with a longer stroke – its fitment necessitated the incorporation of a bulged nosewheel door to fully enclose the wheel. Increased armament in the form of four lower fuselage 'packages', each containing a single 0.50-in machine-gun for use by the pilot, was also introduced on the B-4.

The next major sub-variant introduced by Martin was the B-26B-10, which boasted an extended wing (with a 71-ft span) and an associated increase in wing area to 658 ft^2. A taller fin and rudder were also fitted to both compensate for the greater wing area and improve stability. The B-10's waist gun positions were enlarged and moved further aft, leaving them aligned with the fin leading edge. All these improvements added weight to the Martin bomber, and performance inevitably suffered – the aircraft's top speed dropped below 300 mph to 282 mph at 15,000 ft. Small changes were made on the equivalent Omaha-built B-26C-5 which, aside from its designation, was otherwise similar to the B-26B-10, and entered production slightly ahead of the latter type. These modifications combined to make the Marauder more aerodynamically efficient and stable than before, although the new variants still retained the type's longer fuselage with pointed tail cone and stepped rear gunner's window. The increase in the aircraft's armament now also meant that the B-10/C-5 carried as many guns as a heavy four-engined bomber.

No clearly defined operational plan for attacks on continental targets existed at the time of the arrival of the first B-26 crews of the 322nd BG at Bury St Edmunds, in Suffolk, in December 1942. As a full unit, the group was comprised of the 449th, 450th, 451st and 452nd BSs, in line with standard USAAF composition of heavy, medium and light bomber groups. It was planned that a third wing of the Eighth Air Force would eventually operate no less than 15 groups of 'mediums' from bases in the UK. Despite committing such a large force to this theatre, all that had been decided by USAAF strategists (who based their theories on the experience of B-26 units in the Pacific) was that attacking at low level was believed to be the best way to surprise the German defences. Such zero altitude operations had

From some angles initial production B-26B-10s and C-5s looked similar to early B-series Marauders, but the revised (and centred) rudder trim tab hinge was a reliable clue to a 'big wing/ big tail' aeroplane when viewed on the ground in profile. Omaha-built B-26C-5 41-34678 is shown here shortly after being rolled out of the Martin factory *(MAP)*

been successfully carried out by No 2 Group RAF (although not with Marauders), and a considerable amount of data was on file in England pertaining to the planning and execution of these missions.

Some questions nevertheless remained unanswered, not the least of which was how much crew experience and familiarity with the Marauder would have a bearing on initial mission success. Tasked primarily with rebuilding a strategic bomber force, and making good the strength lost to the Twelfth Air Force in late 1942 following Operation *Torch*, the Eighth was then still learning its trade. Nobody could answer vital questions about medium bomber operations in the ETO before a single mission had been flown, although an historic precedent had been set by a handful of American crews who had undertaken the very first Eighth Air Force bomber sorties in borrowed RAF Bostons in June and July 1942. Another question that festered away in the back of many an aircrewmans' mind in England in 1942/43 was just how safe their B-26 mount really was from a structural standpoint. A spate of training accidents back in the US had led to the bomber picking up disparaging nicknames such as 'Widow Maker' 'Martin Murderer' and 'Baltimore Whore', this last sobriquet alluding to the aircraft's short wing – it had 'no visible means of support'.

In fact the Marauder's training record was not that bad, and was certainly far removed from the wildly exaggerated 'one a day in Tampa Bay' tag which stemmed from the fact that the bomber's main training base at McDill AFB, Florida, had recorded a small number of aircraft going down into the waters of the nearby bay. There certainly hadn't been many such casualties by the time the 322nd arrived in England, for in total only 13 B-26s were lost in this fashion in the 14 months from 5 August 1942, when the first Marauder was lost, to the final operational crash on 8 October 1943.

The Eighth's first B-26 crews (belonging to the 450th BS) embarked on a rigorous theatre training programme beginning in January 1943. The need for such training was clearly obvious, for few pilots assigned to the unit had flown the Marauder in formation before, hardly anyone had experience of low flying and none of the gunners had ever fired a shot in anger. Unfortunately, little operational guidance was offered by senior USAAF strategists either in respect to the ideal bombing altitude B-26 crews should deliver their ordnance from on missions over Europe, or in the number of aircraft to deploy and the formations they should adopt. Therefore, acting 322nd BG CO, Maj Glenn C Nye, was left to hypothesise that if no more than 12 aircraft attacked small targets at low level, the element of surprise should result in good bombing.

Having essentially worked out its own operational tactics, the 450th BS busied itself preparing the 14 'short wing and short tail' B-26B-2s that had arrived at their Suffolk base in March 1943 for combat. And while the adoption of low-level bombing tactics appeared to be a sound decision, the experiences accrued in other theatres could never duplicate the conditions prevailing in the ETO – particularly the strength of German air and ground defences allied with an efficient early warning radar and radio network, the combination of which usually resulted in a swift reaction to any attack.

But as low flying was officially in favour, the Marauder crews carried out the necessary training with considerable enthusiasm. The peaceful countryside around Bury St Edmunds soon reverberated to the roar of Pratt & Whitney Twin Wasp engines as all 4000 hp produced by the paired powerplants on each bomber was unleashed by 'green' crews wringing every ounce of performance out of their Martin mounts. Lightly loaded for practice sorties, the early B-26B-2s (which were joined by B-26B-3s before operations commenced) had an impressive performance. 'Flat out', a lightly-loaded B-26 could top 280 mph, which was a respectable turn of speed for any bomber in 1943. The good folk of Suffolk soon learned to tolerate the sleek olive drab and grey bombers with their cigar-shaped fuselages hedge-hopping at what seemed to them to be phenomenal speeds.

In April 1943 the 452nd BS became the second of the 322nd BG's Marauder squadrons to arrive in the UK. It brought with it B-26B-4s fitted with package guns, and it was soon decided that only these more heavily-armed aircraft would be used on actual combat missions. Arriving at around the same time was new group commander, Col Robert M Stillman. Among the myriad problems awaiting the colonel's attention, perhaps the most pressing was the question of the ideal operating altitude for the B-26 – Stillman finally decided that only combat would resolve it. Selected crews belonging to each squadron were alerted for their debut mission on 14 May.

Since their capture of Holland in 1940, the Germans had integrated various industrial plants into their own war economy, including the PEN generating station at Imjuiden, on the Dutch coast. This plant was chosen as the premier target for the Eighth Air Force's B-26s. At briefing the crews were told that their target approach altitude would be less than 100 ft – in airman's jargon, 'zero feet'. A dozen B-26B-4s were readied for the mission in a frantic hurry, preparations including the removal of the D-8 bomb sight, which was not accurate enough for small targets, and its replacement by a modified N-6 sight – the latter was installed in the cockpit for use by the co-pilot, who also operated a chord cable with a button to release the bomb load.

Apart from the standard frequency changes made to the aircrafts' US radio sets in order to allow them to function efficiently in the ETO, the 322nd's Marauders also had to have IFF radar warning equipment fitted and their compasses relocated in the nose. The latter modification came about because the navigator's position had been moved forward from its normal location behind the flight deck in order to improve his vision during low-level navigation. In addition, each aircraft scheduled for this debut raid was rigged to carry four British 500-lb delayed action (DA) bombs designed to minimise injury to Dutch civilian workers.

Twelve Marauders duly set out from their Suffolk base at 9.50 am to bomb Imjuiden on the morning of 14 May 1943, and apart from one early return, the rest released their load on the power station complex for a seemingly successful operation. All 11 aircraft returned to England, most with damage from ground fire, and Lt John J Howell was killed when his aircraft spun in whilst attempting an emergency landing – the remaining crewmembers survived, however, as Howell had ordered them to bail out once he had made landfall over East Anglia. This loss was a sobering introduction to combat, but at debriefing all crews felt that their bombing had been accurate enough, considering their inexperience.

B-26B-4 *TONDALAYO* was one of the original 322nd BG aircraft to fly the initial Imjuiden mission on 14 May 1943. It missed the disastrous follow up raid on the Dutch power station and survived a subsequent mishap, resulting in the bomber being renamed *Mr Period Twice* – 'nuff said! (*USAF*)

However, a critical analysis of the post-strike target photographs revealed that the power station had suffered virtually no damage. Despite the complex apparently being hit a number of times, the use of British DA bombs was believed to have given the Germans ample time to dispose of them. In reality, only about 18 bombs (out of 43 dropped) had actually hit the target.

Some slight damage was indeed done to power generation when some of these bombs eventually exploded, but the generally disappointing results, now starkly etched on film, caused a follow-up raid on Imjuiden to be planned for just three days after the first one. The same route would be followed, much to the participants' alarm. Despite their newness to combat, 322nd BG crews knew that to return to the same target within a short space of time was inviting disaster, for having been attacked once, the enemy would be alerted to further possible raids, resulting in the inevitable strengthening of local defences. Pessimism held full sway in the messes at Bury St Edmunds when news of the mission was released, and few members of the crews slated to bomb the Dutch power station expected to return to England.

Imjuiden was by no means a fresh target for Allied bombers, and it cannot have escaped the notice of 3rd Wing Intelligence that only two weeks before the 322nd's debut mission, the RAF's No 2 Group had attacked that self-same site, with disastrous results. In a similar 'follow-up' raid on 3 May, an entire formation of No 487 Sqn Lockheed Venturas had been destroyed. The omens were therefore bad, but perhaps it was felt that if the USAAF prevailed where their Allies had failed, the public relations boost would be immense. And there was no denying that at that time, the B-26 needed all the positive publicity it could get.

Led by Col Stillman, 11 Marauders duly took off from Bury St Edmunds at 10.56 am on 17 May, forming up in a 'double javelin' formation before heading east in the direction of the Suffolk coast. The aircraft flown by Capt Stephens had to abort the mission due to mechanical malfunction, while the rest, swinging around to avoid a suspicious convoy, made landfall on the Dutch coast. This detour put the force 18 miles south of the briefed route, and right in the path of a series of coastal flak batteries around the mouth of the river Maas. The German gunners quickly ranged in on the olive drab bombers despite their low altitude.

11

'Moose' Stillman's aircraft was the first to go down – mortally hit, 41-17982 flipped over and hit the ground inverted. Miraculously, three men, including the colonel, were pulled from the resulting wreckage by the German soldiers.

The two B-26 elements ploughed on, making a circuitous target run-in against alerted defences. Lt Garrambone's aircraft was also shot down by flak, with four men surviving the crash. Two aircraft were lost in a collision near to the target, with a third going down after being hit by the resulting debris. This left just one Marauder, piloted by Lt Col William Purinton, to drop its bombs – but not on the Imjuiden power station. He was subsequently forced to ditch his battle-damaged bomber off the Dutch coast, this loss being the fifth, and last, credited to German flak on the ill-fated sortie.

In the meantime the presence of American bombers charging over half of Holland had resulted in an *Alarmstart* at Woensdrecht, then home to JG 1, which sent off 26 Fw 190s to investigate. The two remaining B-26s were detected fleeing for home at wave top height and were both swiftly shot down into the sea, Feldwebel Niedereichholtz of the *Geschwaderstab* and Oberfeldwebel Winkler of 4. *Staffel* being credited with a kill apiece.

Of the 60 men who set out on the second Imjuiden raid, 26 were to survive with varying degrees of injury, including two who were picked up in a life raft 48 hours later by a British destroyer. None were as surprised to have lived through the experience than Robert Stillman, who told his story after the war. Recalling the crash as best he could, he told reporters;

'The ship started to snap-roll. A snap-roll is like a corkscrew. I wasn't scared. I didn't have time to be. But I knew this was curtains. A wing was down. I looked out the side window and saw the ground coming up. There was nothing to do but shut my eyes and wait. It's peculiar that at a time like that a man isn't worried.'

Others were mortified. Lt Col Purinton, upon seeing Stillman walk into the PoW camp (*Stalag Luft III*) they were to share at Sagan, momentarily refused to believe he was alive, let alone mobile. 'You can't be here', exclaimed Purinton. 'You're dead. We saw you crash. I've already reported you and your entire crew as dead'.

More than pleased to be able to contradict that statement, Stillman was also able, by the time he reached the camp, to fill in details pertaining to his amazing escape from death. Other 322nd crewmen who had been in the same hospital were eye-witnesses to Stillman's crash. They said that the colonel's aircraft had seemed to recover momentarily after the first snap-roll, but then had begun to yaw. It half completed a second roll and then crashed.

Stillman himself theorised that when Capt Stephens aborted the mission midway across the Channel, he climbed to about 1000 ft in compliance with B-26 emergency procedure in order to give his crew enough height to bail out if necessary. This, felt Stillman, had exposed Stephens' aircraft to enemy radar, and thus alerted the German operators to the presence of the rest. The B-26s had also been seen off the Dutch coast by

With new 'bars to the star,' and their short-lived red-outline, 41-7995 (now in the guise of *Mr Period Twice*) looks suitably different to the way it appeared on the previous page. The bomb log has increased and the prop hubs appear to have been stripped of paint. The closeness of the individual aircraft code letter to the national insignia illustrates the difficulty squadron painters faced in making the letters readable (*USAF*)

fishing vessels, whose crews undoubtedly radioed that information ashore. Stillman finished by stating that had he known that Stephens had unwittingly 'blown their cover', he might have aborted the entire mission.

Back at Bury St Edmunds, the disconsolate 322nd groundcrews could hardly believe the scale of the disaster as the clocks ticked round past the time that the B-26s could possibly have returned. Rumours began to spread – maybe the B-26 was a jinxed ship and maybe the 322nd was a jinxed outfit. There were many maybes, but few answers.

NEW COMMAND

Officialdom moved quickly after the second Imjuiden raid. By June 1943 the B-26 had been temporarily removed from the Eighth Bomber Command first line Order of Battle and placed under the jurisdiction of Eighth Air Support Command (ASC). Movement of a 'second batch' of B-26 groups to England was halted, and the 3rd Wing was taken over by Col Samuel E Anderson, a Marauder pilot with some experience. He faced a tough job in convincing both the combat crews and higher authority that the B-26 was being unfairly slandered, and that there was no such animal as a jinxed aircraft. As for the second Imjuiden raid, its outcome was just one of the 'fortunes of war', with a scale of loss that was by no means unique on the Channel front.

With movement orders already in motion, it was decided that the three remaining B-26 groups originally slated to join the Eighth would do so – indeed, the first of these, the 323rd, arrived in England just as the 322nd had flown its initial combat missions. Bad news travels fast, and crews within the new group were quickly made aware that their journey may not have been necessary for no new missions were to be flown until the 3rd Wing had either new aircraft or revised tactics – that was the word.

British input on medium bomber operations, plus that from the Mediterranean, where Twelfth Air Force B-26 crews had been obliged by heavy defences to adopt a medium altitude bombing technique, convinced most people that if 3rd Wing was to continue to operate the Marauder, it had little choice but to give medium altitude bombing a try.

With the arrival of Col Anderson, and the wing's reassignment to ASC, the Eighth's B-26 groups vacated their Suffolk airfields and moved further south to bases in Essex. Group command of the 322nd reverted to Lt Col Glenn Nye following the loss of Robert Stillman, and the unit moved to Great Saling, or 'Andrews Field' as the Americans renamed it. The 323rd BG, with its 453rd, 454th, 455th and 456th BSs under the command of Col Herbert B Thatcher, went to Earls Colne. The third Marauder group to arrive was Col Richard C Sanders' 386th BG (552nd, 553rd, 554th and 555th BSs), which was stationed at Boxted. The fourth, and last (for the time being at least) outfit sent to Essex was the 387th BG (556th, 557th, 558th and 559th BSs), commanded by Col Carl R Storrie, which would be based at Chipping Ongar.

The move south placed a whole host of new targets within the 300-mile radius of action enjoyed by the Marauder force. Henceforth, the majority of operations undertaken by 3rd Wing B-26s would see bombs dropped from medium altitudes ranging between 10,000 to 15,000 ft. An intensive training programme to help bombardiers get used to aiming from these altitudes (as well as to allow pilots and co-pilots to operate their aircraft in close formation) was put in hand as soon as the groups had settled into their new surroundings.

Back in the US, Marauder production was in a state of transition as frontline units in the ETO changed their operational procedures, resulting in squadrons being equipped with a variety of sub-types. For example, the 323rd had brought over Omaha-built B-26C-6s configured for single-pilot operation in line with low-level attack doctrine, but with this now ruled out, these machines had perforce to be modified back to standard pilot/co-pilot operation. Although some of these aircraft were used operationally, the majority were relegated to second line and training duties, pending the delivery of new Marauders from the US. This was also the lot of the remaining original short wing and tail B-26s.

The 322nd BG's remaining two squadrons brought over the first 'big wing' B-26B-10s and Cs to be seen in the ETO, and the force would soon standardise on these improved aircraft – most crews did, however, note that the new Marauders weighed around 2000 lbs more than the older models, and were slower accordingly. Switching to bombing from a higher altitude also required new equipment, particularly the Norden M series bombsight – an item absent on all B-26s up to this point in the war.

In the meantime crews improvised, honing their formation flying skills and standardising on a three-ship vic, two of which formed a flight of six and three of the latter an eighteen-ship box. Staggered flights within each box gave the gunners maximum fields of fire, the formation being based on those adopted by AAF heavy bombers. Fighter cover was considered essential for medium bomber operations, and with no US escorts to spare, the B-26 crews found themselves comfortingly surrounded by hordes of RAF Spitfires. The Americans were highly appreciative of their fighter protection, which generally kept the Luftwaffe at bay. Joint discussions had led to an initial fighter-to-bomber ratio as generous as four-to-one, a figure that later had to be modified both in light of Fighter Command's own commitments and the increasing number of B-26s. By July 1943, the 16 Marauder squadrons allocated to Eighth ASC had been issued with roughly 300 B-26Bs and Cs.

ROUND TWO

On 16 July 1943, some eight weeks after the true debut of the B-26 in the ETO, the 3rd BW initiated its first medium altitude mission. This was also the first combat mission for the 323rd BG, which sent 18 aircraft to bomb the Abbeville marshalling yards – 14 Marauders were able to drop just under 17 tons of bombs on tracks and installations, and while flak damaged ten aircraft, all of them came home. This safe return to base was anticipated just as much as the two Imjuiden raids had been, and undoubtedly many silent prayers were offered up before the first B-26s appeared over Earl's Colne. This time, the prayers were answered.

A diversionary mission was flown the following day, and Spitfires escorted 18 B-26s of the 323rd to attack the coke ovens at Ghent on the 25th. Subsequent operations were also against airfields and coke ovens, crews taking advantage of good weather to further hone their revised technique.

The first mission flown by 'The Crusaders' of the 386th BG was performed early on the morning of 30 July. Covered by eight squadrons of Spitfires, the group was briefed to attack the Luftwaffe fighter airfield at Woensdretch, Holland, and sent 24 Marauders off from Boxted in compliance with the Field Order. An otherwise smooth take-off by aircraft of all four squadrons was marred by the crash-landing of *Two Way Ticket* of the 533rd BS, which lost power on one engine almost immediately after launching. Its pilot, 1Lt Williamson, skilfully put the bomber down in a field, the force of the crash shearing off both engines and breaking the fuselage in two. Miraculously, all the crew survived, with Lt Williamson's broken finger being the worst injury sustained.

Having made their rendezvous with the Spitfire escort over Ordfordness, the B-26s proceeded to the target at 11,000 ft, with the fighters some 5000 ft above them. Some aircraft of the 552nd and 553rd flights picked up a few holes from light flak en route, but no aircraft were shot down.

Radio traffic had alerted the German airfields within range of the Marauders, and eight Fw 190As of 2./JG 26 were scrambled from Grimbergen in anticipation of action. Executing a rapid 'hit and run' attack, using the bomber formation to shield them from the Spitfires, the Focke-Wulfs scored a number of telling hits on the tightly-packed Marauders. Lt Karl 'Charlie' Willius bored in and sent 1Lt Glenn Zimmerman's B-26 (coincidentally nicknamed *The Wolf*) down with an engine smoking. Gunners responded admirably to the threat, and 9000 rounds were quickly fired from the barrels of the massed .50 cal machine-guns – enough to destroy one of the Luftwaffe fighters in an action that lasted less than a minute.

On returning to England the inexperienced crews of the 386th understandably assessed the mission differently. It was universally reckoned to have been a rough one, the gunners being credited with six enemy fighters destroyed, plus six probables – it was a near-impossibility to accurately gauge such claims in the heat of battle. Overall, the air battle was also estimated to have lasted a full three minutes, and involved at least 15 Fw 190s and Bf 109s. Luftwaffe Intelligence gave a more realistic appraisal of the combat, although the single credit awarded to Willius for his victory reflected the rarity of claims against Marauders, for it went into German records as a 'Boston'.

Less than half (11 out of 23) of the B-26s despatched by the group dropped their 300-lb GP bombs on Woensdrecht due to ground haze and sighting difficulties. Damage to the airfield was consequently slight, whilst the occupants of Coutrai were spared any inconvenience at all from American bombs as their would-be antagonists (the 323rd BG) were forced to turn for home after their escort reported that the target airfields were fogbound.

'The Crusaders' would later put their debut mission into perspective, and apart from having the dubious distinction of losing the first Marauder on medium altitude operations in the ETO, come to realise that missions could be far rougher than that of 30 July 1943. But perhaps the most sobering event of the day had little to do with this first mission. A badly shot up B-17 put down at Boxted later that afternoon, and 386th skipper, Lt Col Lester Maitland, offered to fly the crew back to their base. They refused point blank, saying that they would rather face the Luftwaffe than ride in a B-26!

HONING THE TECHNIQUE

On 15 August the B-26Bs of the 387th BG flew their first mission from Chipping Ongar. The group's crews were more than eager to put their first operational sorties behind them, having been frustrated in their attempts to achieve this milestone for several weeks because of the weather. St Omer/Ft Rouge airfield was the object of their attention, and crews were treated

to a graphic demonstration of the accuracy of German flak. By making a long, straight, bombing run, the 387th exposed itself to plenty of 'flying steel', and upon their return to Essex, no less than 18 of the 36 B-26s despatched were found to have suffered damage. Target approach techniques were rapidly revised.

When 3rd BW HQ finally circulated an operational plan for its four B-26 groups, it confirmed that in general, medium altitude bombing would henceforth be the order of the day. Low-level attacks by Marauders was not entirely ruled out, but would depend on the target – anti-shipping strikes were also to be flown, and night bombing would be studied. In the event, the 322nd was to continue flying at lower altitudes, while the 323rd, 386th and 387th concentrated on medium bombing.

As the bomber groups' principal weapon, the B-26B could carry up to 4800 lbs of ordnance in maximum overload configuration, which generally consisted of 16 300-lb HE bombs – heavier loads were usually reserved for short range missions to targets on, or near, the French coast. A more typical maximum load was four 1000-lb or eight 500-lb bombs. In practise, however, Marauders usually flew missions below full ordnance weight in order to avoid a deterioration in handling and performance. Typical loads included 12 300-lb HE bombs totalling 3600 lbs,

One of the first press announcements noting the operation of USAAF B-26s from bases in Britain was made on 19 August 1943. Cameramen took candid views of groundcrews carrying out their daily routine around the B-26s of the 456th BS at Earls Colne, which had been home to the 323rd BG for almost a month. Parked behind the Marauder awaiting its next call is an Airspeed Oxford, one of the more useful 'runabouts' loaned to the Americans by the RAF (*via Aeroplane*)

With its code letters freshly applied, B-26B VT-K of the 453rd BS makes a dramatic take-off from Earls Colne in mid-1943. As one of the few bombers actually authorised to charge around the English countryside at 'zero feet', the Marauder was often seen at tree-top height over Essex in 1943. Few who witnessed the fast landings and take-offs associated with the Martin bomber ever forgot the impression they made – 'hot' ships they certainly were (*via Aeroplane*)

20 100-lb incendiaries (total 2000 lbs) or 26 100-lb incendiaries (2600 lbs). Mixed loads of HE, incendiary and fragmentation were also utilised, and when the target demanded it, a pair of 2000-lb GPs could be carried.

Various bombing methods were adopted depending on the type of target. For instance, by opening out the formation immediately before release, a B-26 group carrying 250-lb fragmentation clusters could devastate a column of troops or a convoy of soft-skinned vehicles. At the other extreme, a compact target such as a bridge required precision bombing techniques – the latter were to become a B-26 speciality. AAF target planners and photo interpreters worked long and hard with reconnaissance shots of bridges, which, taken in conjunction with intelligence reports from the ground, determined their structure, and the bomb load necessary to ensure their destruction. Good bombing also relied on correct fusing, the delayed action type often being used against bridge supports.

The debut of the 387th BG was another encouraging demonstration for the numerous pro-Marauder elements within the Eighth, as the addition of the new crews from Chipping Ongar meant that the 3rd BW was now able to marshal the strength of nearly three full groups. Although the 386th had been obliged to turn back at the Dutch coast on 15 August, the waxing power of the ETO B-26 force was shown by that fact that no less than 93 aircraft had taken off on the three missions planned for that day.

Two days later, on the first anniversary of the commencement of the Eighth Air Force's daylight bombing campaign from England, the USAAF carried out a double raid on Schweinfurt and Regensburg which resulted in the bloodiest air battles yet seen over Europe. Under somewhat smaller headlines, the 3rd BW set another record by sending out more than 100 B-26s for the first time.

Charged with taking some of the heat off the 'heavies', all three Marauder groups despatched 36 aircraft apiece to bomb French fighter

A fair number of the B-26s assigned mainly to the 449th BS had a unique 'three-tone' camouflage scheme, which served to break up the fuselage outline – it was reminiscent of the experimental 'sea search' schemes tried out in the US. It did not last much beyond a major overhaul, however, when groundcrews took the chance to repaint squadron aircraft in the more manageable shades of olive drab ('OD') and grey (*USAF*)

bases used by the *Jagdwaffe*. The 387th was, however, recalled by their escort en route because of bad weather over the target. On the 19th each group again despatched 36 B-26s to raid French airfields, and this time it was the 322nd that could not bomb due to cloud obscuring Bryas Sud.

Prior to the 387th BG being declared operational, newly-promoted Gen Anderson had provided a portent of things to come when, on 28 July, he had sortied B-26s of the 323rd BG twice in one day. Another significant change was also made 24 hours later when the group added a further element of three aircraft to its standard box formation, this new figure of 21 Marauders soon being boosted further to 24. The summer offensive would continue along these established lines, the combat diary of the B-26 force in August/September including the following targets:

20 August – airfields at Poix and Amiens-Ghissy

31 August – airfields at St Omer and Lille-Vendeville, and a power station at Manzigure

3 September – Manziburbe power station and targets in Pas de Calais

6 September – Marshalling yards at Ghent, in Belgium.

On the majority of missions, photographic reconnaissance showed that tactical targets needed hitting repeatedly as the Germans were more than adept at effecting rapid repairs to airfields, installations, factories and marshalling yards deemed important to their war effort. Due to the enemy's effective repair techniques, it became difficult to assess the lasting results of bombing factories and power stations with a small weight of high explosive, but the B-26s nevertheless helped to maintain the pressure on the Germans by causing widespread disruption rather than total destruction. It was felt that while medium bombers couldn't break the enemy's will to resist, they could sap his effectiveness by attacking on a broad front near-daily. Luftwaffe commanders had to constantly juggle fighter availability rates in the light of destruction and damage to aircraft, runways and dispersals.

Damage wrought by 3rd BW B-26s was added to that already being dished out by the medium and light bombers of the RAF. As the number of Marauder missions increased, so the flak appeared (at least to the crews) to multiply accordingly!

Making their way along the taxy strip at 'Andrews Field' (Great Saling) in September 1943, these 322nd BG Marauders prepare to embark on yet another bombing raid againts French airfields in August 1943 – each group could launch as many as 36 bombers at a time depending on serviceability rates. Leading this line up is a B-26B-20 marked with two white ducks under its cockpit, thus symbolising its participation in decoy sorties flown in association with larger heavy bomber raids into Germany. These missions were part and parcel of the B-26's phase of operations under Eighth Air Support Command *(USAF)*

Taxying Marauders over grass must have given some pilots a few anxious moments, for the aircraft was occasionally prone to suffering nosewheel strut failure. However, most airfields used by B-26 groups were RAF Class A sites, with paved runways and taxyways. The Martin production block which included this B-26B-15 amongst its ranks was the last to feature the stepped tail gun position with hand-held twin 'fifties' *(USAF)*

Bat Outa Hell II was a name many people might have chosen for the fast B-26. Col Carl Storrie, CO of the 387th BG, got in first, however, and he liked 'his' Marauder so much that he took it with him to Earls Colne when he was promoted to command the 98th BW. Considering wartime attrition rates, few officers would have believed that many of these same aircraft would survive through to VE-Day having flown record numbers of sorties – the *'Bat* eventually flew 144 missions. Few other Allied bombers could match the B-26 in this respect (*USAF*)

Anti-aircraft fire was seen as *the* major threat to 'mediums', and few escaped being hit. One of the most important sections on B-26 bases was the sheet metal shop, whose personnel were kept busy patching aircraft and, where necessary, cutting whole sections from 'hanger queens' and using them to keep their brethren flying.

A feature of the 'big wing' Marauders was the factory-addition of applique steel plating, riveted to the outer fuselage on the port side under the cockpit to protect the pilot. Work was put in hand at English bases to add a second plate to the starboard side to similarly shield the co-pilot from deadly splinters of steel. This armour took on a secondary purpose as crews used it as a location for the aircraft's bomb log, nose-art and nicknames. To further minimise injuries from shrapnel, the crews were issued with standard GI-pattern helmets and body armour – enough 'flak suits' had arrived in the ETO by late August to equip every B-26 crewman.

Each Marauder was equipped with a K-12 strike camera in the waist position to record bombing results, and other less palatable occurrences. An example of the latter occurred on 31 August when 387th BG crews brought back an unhappy memento of the mission – a photo record of the demise of one of their number, cut completely in half by a direct flak hit aft of the bomb bay some 11,000 ft over Lille/Vendeville airfield. It was not the last time that aerial cameras would record the demise of a B-26.

Gunnery steadily improved, and combat soon revealed which of the Marauder's five (nose, two waist, turret and tail) defensive positions was the most effective against fighters. Marksmanship varied with the experience of the individual crew member, and although the 'best pattern' was achieved by the Browning M2 at 250 yards, correctly estimating the range of an attacking fighter, and patiently waiting for the right moment to commence firing, was not always practised – gunners would blaze away, often when an enemy fighter was way out of range. However, the deterrent factor of an interlacing web of fire was considerable, particularly as German pilots themselves often had difficulty in estimating range. They too were prone to opening fire from much too far out.

Regarding the effectiveness of the Marauder's defensive guns, the Martin dorsal turret, with its superb, almost unobstructed, visibility, and the powered tail gun position won every time, the waist guns proving the least accurate owing to their limited fields of fire. In any event, hand-held guns in bombers were very much on the way out, although they were occasionally effective and certainly boosted morale. There were few more satisfying ways for a bomber crewman to feel he was fighting back when enemy aircraft attacked than to put a heavy machine gun into his hands!

And that is not to say that a lucky burst of fire could not 'nail' a fighter attacking from below, for the B-26's waist guns could fire vertically downwards, and the destructive power of a .50 cal machine-gun was always formidable. But the sheer rarity of the *Jadgwaffe* getting 'too close for comfort' usually led flight crews to call the waist gunners forward first if they required any help.

Wounded crewmen aboard a Marauder derived some solace from the fact that bombers carried an ample first aid kit. This contained a web belt tourniquet, sulphur tablets and powder for dusting open wounds, a morphine syringe and assorted bandages. Such simple, but

effective, aids offered some relief from the pain prior to the wounded receiving expert help back at base. Thousands of crewmen owed their lives to timely medical attention from comrades while the mission was still in progress.

British fighter escort continued to be the most effective deterrent to *Jagdwaffe* attacks on B-26 formations. There were some missed rendezvous with the fighters mainly owing to Europe's changeable weather conditions, but in the main the escort could be relied upon. Diversionary raids and recalls occasionally gave the crews anxious moments if their aircraft had to land with full bomb bays, which some were obliged to do.

Poor weather could also result in some impromptu bomb aiming practice. If the target was 'socked in' the bombs would alternatively be jettisoned over recognised ranges, whilst occasionally the Spitfires were able to save Marauder crews a wasted journey by turning the bombers back from a cloud-covered target before they had flown too far over enemy territory. The latter helped foster a good working relationship between the two Allied air forces, and a comment on relations between B-26 crews and Spitfire pilots was given by one 3rd BW group CO;

'When an RAF pilot drops in here and we take him up to the bar for a drink, we only pay for our own – drinks for the RAF are on the house. Guess that's why all the Spitfires seem to give out of gas over our field, which is okay with us.'

For their own protection on combat missions, the Marauder groups tried to be as self-sufficient as possible. The value of adopting evasive action in the target area as standard procedure was both well understood and frequently demonstrated when flak bursts came near to, but clear of, aircraft that had been occupying that exact spot moments before. Evasion primarily involved a change of course or a variation in altitude every 20 seconds, AAF Intelligence having learned that it took a German gun crew 30 seconds to re-set their weapons for any range change by their potential target.

While known continental flak 'hot spots' were avoided during mission planning, the medium altitude

Nose to tail, B-26s of the 451st BS are seen taxying out at 'Andrews Field', with *Pickled Dilly* the second Marauder in line. Just visible on the nosewheel hub is a five-pointed star – a not uncommon decoration on USAAF medium bombers. This aircraft also went on to complete 100 missions, but was shot down while flying its 106th sortie (a night raid) on 8 July 1944 (*USAF*)

Once the Marauder had flown a few dozens missions with the Eighth, and thus defied the prediction from some quarters that it would be shot out of the sky, the aircraft truly came into its own with the newly-created Ninth Air Force. Aircraft like this early B-model (41-31606), nick-named *Rat Poison* and assigned to the 386th BG, and a number of others like her took on the mantle of unit 'mascots' as a result of their impressive mission tallies. On a visit to the B-17-equipped 381st BG at Ridgewell, Essex, Lt F W Harris' mount gave little hint to the fact that a further 106 sorties would be flown by the Martin 'twin' (*USAF*)

adopted by Marauder formations could be little short of lethal if a substantial number of guns were sited around a target. Crews often had to sit there and take it, for once committed to the bomb run, they could not deviate far off track for fear of missing the target completely, or breaking the continuity of the combat box and spreading the bombing ineffectually. Despite this, relatively few B-26s (or indeed other bombers) were totally destroyed by a direct hit.

For the Marauder crews themselves, the bombing campaign during the second half of 1943 was executed with encouragingly modest losses. German fighters had, on occasion, penetrated the escort screen and shot down some bombers, but stout formation-keeping, coupled with the B-26's good performance and heavy defensive armament, all combined to turn in some of the best sortie-to-loss ratios in the ETO.

Encouraging as the low losses were, the *raison d'être* of the B-26 gave cause for some concern, for the accuracy of the bombing had been very poor at times, and a substantial number of civilians living near to the targets had paid with their lives when American ordnance went wide. Such errors were classified as 'short' (in front of the target) or 'long' (over the target) bombing. With bombardiers obviously unable to take full advantage of the potentially high destructive yield offered by a tight box formation of laden B-26s, the 3rd BW decided to adopt B-17 group tactics by introducing the bomb-on-leader technique – it was first used on 2 September when the Mazingarbe generating station in Belgium was attacked.

Bombing accuracy soon improved, coupled with a crew survival rate (calculated at the end of August 1943) of 37.35 missions for a B-26, against 17.74 for a B-17. Few could argue with figures like that, and they helped bury the Marauder's previously poor reputation.

Changes were now afoot, however, as the B-26 force was to be transferred to a new tactical air arm – the Ninth Air Force. By the time its service with the Eighth came to an end on 9 October 1943, the Marauder had been alerted for operations by Field Order on 83 occasions, with all but two of these missions being directed by ASC.

As the most experienced group, the 322nd had flown 32 of these missions, while the 387th had completed 29 before the Ninth assumed control. The last target tackled during this phase was Woensdrecht airfield – the 323rd and 387th BGs despatched 72 aircraft, of which 66 were able to bomb. As 'Hap' Arnold put it, 'The Marauder has found its place in the sun'.

Months later, and Rat Poison has dramatically increased its mission tally. The aircraft went on to fly 164 combat sorties, yet never had a 'half and half' paint strip down like other veteran B-26s. Instead, she remained looking much like she'd always done, and was retained even after the 386th had converted to Invaders (T Bivens)

Few aircraft invloved in World War 2 on either side had such superb streamlining as the B-26, and features introduced by Martin on its most famous product would be emulated everywhere. Posing either at home or on diversion at a B-17 base, Tootsie (41-34787) served as WT-P with the 456th BS (USAF)

THE NEW NINTH

On 16 October 1943 the US Ninth Army Air Force, which had existed in the Mediterranean for 15 months, was reconstituted in England as a new tactical force to support the forthcoming invasion of continental Europe. It took over the four groups of B-26s (totalling some 225 machines) from Eighth ASC, and would receive additional groups of medium and attack bombers, fighters, reconnaissance aircraft and transports in due course. In the meantime, the quartet of Marauder groups represented the sole striking power of the new air force, their missions now being directed by the old 3rd BW, which had been reconstituted as Ninth Bomber Command.

Although the Marauder had done well as a tactical bomber in the ETO since transferring to Eighth ASC, it was still viewed with little enthusiasm in official AAF circles. A secret report comparing the performance of the B-26 with the B-25 in North Africa had shown the Marauder to be less effective than the Mitchell in that theatre of operations, and it was hardly the first choice of senior commanders within the Ninth to act as a spearhead for the medium bomber force. Thoughts of its first disastrous missions with Eighth Bomber Command had not endeared the type to some officers, and most were mindful of the Marauder's still poor reputation. On the other hand, many of the men who had actually *flown* the B-26 in combat knew its qualities. They did their best to defend a fine aircraft although their comments often appeared to fall on deaf ears – bad reputations have a habit of sticking. Army Boards of Investigation began probing the Marauder's combat record.

It was certainly true that although the B-26 was perfectly safe in experienced hands, it had a high performance and landing speed and was therefore not considered to be a particularly forgiving aircraft, thus mak-

Although enjoying superb all-round vision when he was hunched over the sight, a B-26 bombardier hardly had the nose area to himself. Two guns, ammunition boxes, and their belts of large shells, made the place a little cluttered. One of the guns (not uncommonly both of them) was removed when the risk of Luftwaffe fighter attack lessened in mid-1944. Under the optically flat panel for bomb aiming was a window to get rid of the shell cases (*USAF*)

Open waist hatches with hand-held guns were really relics of the past that arguably had no place on modern bombers like the Marauder. Nevertheless, they were retained right through to VE-Day, being occasionally used to some effect, although the man posing in this view is not what he seems – a German airman, probably a fighter pilot, is seen inside a downed B-26 getting a gunner's eye view of what it must have been like to blaze away at Fw 190s and Bf 109s! (*Bundesarchiv No 65 6325*)

ing it a handful for the novice pilot. The Marauder always landed fast, the correct technique being to make a nosewheel high landing by holding the latter up and maintaining 125 mph well over the airfield boundary. It the early days, noseovers had been common when the rookie pilot applied the brakes too enthusiastically – the B-26's brakes were power-assisted, and thus and very effective. Even experienced

A 451st BS B-26B is seen just prior to its six crew members clambering aboard into their respective positions, strapping in and firing up the engines. A modest mission log adorns *L'il Po'kchop*, although this would soon be extended to total 100 completed sorties by June 1944 (*Crow*)

pilots were caught out by them, as fighter ace Don Lopez found to his embarrassment. He was destined to fly the Marauder only briefly as a test pilot, and he found no problem with it apart from the brakes. A number of Army pilots successfully transitioned from fighters to bombers before war's end, and at first they often applied too much toe pressure when try to slow down or stop – much to the amusement of their wily crew chiefs.

Such problems were addressed, and generally solved, largely through pilot application and the constant refinement of the training syllabus taught to crews prior to them being sent overseas. The introduction of twin-engined types into the American training curriculum also made a great deal of difference. Such aircraft proved to be the 'missing link' between single-engined trainers and operational 'twins', thus removing the very real problem that pilots initially faced during their transition to the B-26.

Martin had, in the meantime, determined the reasons for the bomber's early faults and duly remedied most of them on the pro-

Misty English mornings rapidly lost their charm for young Americans when the daily round meant getting up just to go out and be shot at! At Marauder bases such as Earl's Colne, custom-made covers prevented that all-pervading damp from getting into turret and gun mechanisms. Here, aircraft of the 453rd BS await the fuel bowser as two members of the flight crew, rather than groundmen, prepare their bomber's primary defensive position for combat (*John Hamlin via R MacKay*)

duction line. This was done in the shadow of four separate Board of Investigation hearings convened to discuss the role (if any) of the B-26. For a time, cancellation was a distinct possibility, but with all war theatres crying out for more tactical bombers, terminating the Marauder programme would have needed more justification in the face of a steadily improving combat record and an overall low loss rate. With the B-25 Mitchell as the only other US medium, the A-20 operating solely as an attack bomber and the A-26 Invader (the intended A-20/B-26 replacement) many months from its first ETO deployment due to slipping production schedules, the AAF would have been hard pressed to make good any shortfall created by cancelling the B-26. Fortunately, as subsequent events were to prove, the Marauder more than proved its detractors wrong.

NINTH SPEARHEAD

The Marauder groups of Ninth Bomber Command intended to fly operations in much the same way as they had when part of the Eighth, and

AVM Trafford Leigh Mallory pauses during a visit to Boreham, home of the 386th BG, to chat to one of the ground crew who kept *The Yankee Guerilla* 'spick and span'. The British air chief was photographed during his pre-invasion inspection tour of Allied airfields (*USAF*)

similar to those flown by No 2 Group, RAF. Although this particular British tactical air command had no Marauder units, it had been modernised around the B-25, the A-20 and the Mosquito. The Lend-Lease American types in the RAF enjoyed a range and performance similar to their US counterparts, but when flown as a straight-forward medium bomber, the B-26 offered a significant increase in capability in certain areas when compared with the B-25 or A-20.

The AAF had, in the meantime, decided not to base its own B-25 units in Britain but keep them instead in the Mediterranean alongside the B-26 groups of the Twelfth Air Force and the Marauder squadrons of the RAF and South African Air Force. Thus, all three twin-engined US medium/attack bombers saw service in the ETO/MTO, albeit with different air arms.

For the medium bomber groups still undergoing training in the US on the Marauder, the anticipation of an overseas combat tour tended to put rumours into perspective – not everyone took too much heed of the stories that stated that the B-26 was a jinxed ship, being both difficult to fly and downright dangerous. New crews destined for service with the Ninth AAF also remembered the 'good' news that the Marauder was *the* 'hot ship' in the months after Pearl Harbor, performing great deeds in the Pacific. This was the bomber that had shown Japanese fighters – even the much-vaunted Mitsubishi A6M Zero – a clean pair of heels. That kind of thing was remembered just as much as the scuttlebutt about crashes.

Many pilots also appreciated a good turn of speed in the bomber they would fly in combat, and few could deny that the B-26 could outpace most other USAAF 'bombing twins'. Generally speaking, their faith was not misplaced. During the Ninth's build-up in preparation for supporting the greatest invasion the world had ever known, the Marauder continued to confound the rumour mongers by operating successfully in what was widely acknowledged to be the toughest theatre of them all.

Launching its initial medium bomber missions on 18 October, the Ninth sent the 322nd BG to bomb two French airfields – these strikes were followed up four days later with a further raid. The latter mission proved to be very eventful for the six Marauders that were intercepted by 36 Bf 109Gs over Cambrai-Epinoy. Despite being outnumbered, by the formidable enemy force, the B-26 crews beat off their assailants without losing any aircraft – US gunners claimed a modest three probables.

An escort of P-38s was arranged for the 36 Marauders briefed to bomb Montdidier airfield on 24 October, this being the first time that the Lightning had carried out such a task in the ETO. Doubtless the bomber

Flightline scene at 'Andrews Field', with Marauders of the 452nd BS being prepared by the hard-working groundcrews. Note how the grey paint used to pick out the code letters has become almost illegible against the streaked and weathered camouflage of the fuselage. This aircraft has also had the red 'star and bar' surround over-painted with fresh insignia blue, giving it an unusually dark outline (*D Brett via MacKay*)

crews were pleased at the presence of American 'little friends', as the Luftwaffe fighters were again active – 40 of them making a recorded 54 passes at the 'mediums'. Although the *Jagdflieger* failed to bring down a single Marauder, alert bomber gunners claimed 3-3-6.

In November, the Ninth regrouped its B-26 units into Combat Bomb Wings (CBWs), each of which was to have two experienced groups and two new ones assigned – the 98th CBW had the 322nd and 387th, and would get the 394th and 397th, while the 99th CBW would have the experienced 323rd and 386th, along with the new 344th and 391st. The additional groups would not go operational until 1944.

Under the *Pointblank* directive, the Eighth Air Force began a systematic wearing down of the Luftwaffe fighter arm, striking at factories that produced fighters and components, modification centres and airfields. By hunting the *Jagdwaffe* in the air and on the ground through the use of fighters in the dual escort/ground strafing roles, the Eighth aimed to take the pressure off its 'heavies' until such time as they could be accompanied by escorts to the most distant of targets.

The Ninth's contribution to *Pointblank* was to add the weight of its bombs to the destruction already being meted out to the forward German airfields. B-26 crews had 'cut their teeth' bombing airfields, and they continued to perfect their technique against this type of target for some months to come. Repeat visits to tactical targets were deemed necessary due mainly to the near-impossibility of causing lasting damage to grass or concrete runways. With intercepting fighters needing very little space in which to take off, bomb crater-filling had become almost a ground trade in itself on many Luftwaffe airfields!

On 3 October two Marauder groups attacked the Dutch airfield at Schipol. Bombs were released at around 1400 hrs, the main concentration falling on, or near, the hangars, runways and the Fokker workshops. A group of Bf 109Gs took off shortly before the raid but failed to intercept the B-26s, the latter being left to run the gauntlet of the notoriously heavy flak in Holland. Miraculously, no aircraft were brought down.

'BUZZ BOMBS'

Almost three weeks after the formation of the Ninth Air Force, British photographic interpreters discovered a series of strange structures in the Pas de Calais, near Abbeville. Agents confirmed that the Germans were indeed constructing buildings that had one end curved, and when viewed from the air looked like giant skis. Eight 'ski sites' were initially identified, then 19, then 26 – by late November 1943, PR coverage put the number of confirmed sites at 95. Rumours that these buildings were connected with pilotless aircraft (the V1 flying bomb) persisted.

Allied air commanders were taking no chances. Operation *Crossbow* encompassed the entire campaign to wipe out the V-weapons programme. Launching sites for the V1 were generally identified by the code name *Noball*, although for aircrews, this extended to the massive earthworks at Mimoyecques, near Cap Griz Nez, associated with the V3 long range guns. At that time medium bomber crews knew little about what they were bombing – 'special targets' was about all their intelligence officers could divulge.

Sited uncomfortably close to England, the V-weapon sites soon became well defended by flak, and although the Marauder crews neither had far to fly to reach these targets, or had to stay over them for long once there, the missions were rarely viewed as 'milk runs'.

The V1 weapon itself was finally identified on 28 November, and thereafter launching sites were deluged with high explosive dropped by both USAAF and RAF tactical

and heavy bombers. Widespread destruction was caused, leading the enemy to abandon the original ski sites and establish a revised type of launching ramp, first detected near Cherbourg. Again, these new sites were relentlessly attacked, resulting in *Noball* missions providing a considerable chunk of the combat hours flown by Ninth Bomber Command in the lead up to D-Day – so much so that far from a rain of V1s disrupting the invasion, not one was fired in anger until 13 June 1944.

During *Crossbow* most Allied bomber types were used, with the B-26 achieving results comparable with those accrued by 'heavies' like the B-17 or the RAF's more cost-effective Mosquito. A Flying Fortress needed to drop an average of 195.1 tons of bombs to inflict Category A (destroyed) damage on 30 sites, while the Marauder's average was 223.5 tons to destroy 26 sites – the Mosquitos destroyed 19.5 sites with an average of just 39.3 tons. As part of the enormous Allied air effort, the Ninth's medium bomber groups lost 30 aircraft during the first phase (pre-D-Day) of *Crossbow*.

The almost round-the-clock nature of the sorties flown by the four Ninth AF B-26 groups in November and December 1943 is graphically illustrated by the mission rate generated by them – some 1790 effective sorties were flown for the loss of just eight aircraft.

Along with *Noball* targets, missions to more conventional locations associated with the German war effort also occupied the B-26 crews during the closing weeks of 1943, with all four groups making a return visit to Schipol on 13 December. This time the notoriously heavy flak concentration around Amsterdam made it a costly raid, the guns hacking

A classic study of a scene that was repeated thousands of times over between 1943 and 1945 as airpower paved the way for the Allied drive across Europe into Germany itself. Although the 323rd BG (known as the 'White Tails') complied with the late 1943 AAF directive to drop camouflage paint, field commanders felt that their 'naked' aircraft were too visible from above, so a top surface coating of OD was often left on tactical bombers. Releasing their loads of 500-pounders are two aircraft from the 456th BS (*USAF*)

down one aircraft apiece from the 322nd, 323rd and 386th BGs – only the 387th succeeded in bringing all of its aircraft home. Most of the 213 surviving participants had to have their airframes patched up before flying their next missions.

A graphic account of that 13 December raid to Schipol was written by Kenneth J Brown of the 322nd BG, and is reproduced here with some additional editing;

'We've been in England now for some six months. Our medium bombardment group began delivering bombs to Hitler's Third Reich in July. We are awakened rudely. It's five in the morning and very cold in our unheated barracks. We have been alerted for one more mission. We dress quickly and race off to our combat mess. Ernie Pyle liked our mess. He came to visit us, lived in our barracks and wrote about our group (and yours truly) in his book *Brave Men*. Combat crews ate well – there was always the joke, "The condemned men ate a hearty meal".

'After a quick breakfast, we go to the briefing room. The entire front of it is one large map of Europe. Red thread held in place by tacks tells us our mission for today. One look is enough. We know. We have been there before. Its the airfield at Amsterdam – Schipol. The Germans defended it with a passion the last time we were there. They will do the same today.

'The famous "yellow nose" squadron (JG 26) will be defending. I had one chance to shoot down one of those. My gun jammed after one burst. I watched that pilot hosing our planes, killing one of my buddies. Our colonel does a good job at the briefing. He always does. All the important details to remember – weather, altitude, bomb load, fighter penetration - and what to expect.

'Off to the ready room. We sack our valuables. A flyer carries only his dogtags, a photo of himself in civilian clothes (just in case) and his government-issue .45 pistol. An escape kit is sewed into our coveralls with map, compass, a candy bar and some pills – pain killers.

'We gather up our heavy flying gear and head for the bomber. Our crew chief has been there for hours. My pilot talks to the crew chief. Since I'm the radio operator, I talk to the ground radio man. Our bomber is ready. It's a Martin B-26. Weight, 18 tons; bomb load 4000 lbs; 1000 gallons of gasoline. Speed, lean cruise 200 mph – diving to 350 mph. Ours is one of the rare single-control type – we have no co-pilot. Our crew: pilot, nav, bombardier, aerial engineer, radio operator and

Although having initially borrowed an extensive amount of ground equipment from their RAF hosts upon their arrived in England, Army Air Force units quickly became inundated with fine US-made equipment such as the big capacity fuel bowser seen in the foreground of this shot. Behind the truck is B-26B-35 41-31976 of the 450th BS, fully fuelled up and ready for its next mission from 'Andrews Field' (*D Brett via MacKay*)

Identified by yellow triangle tail markings on its B-26s, the Matching-based 391st BG was the fifth Marauder-equipped group to join the Ninth Air Force, going operational in February 1944. On some occasions targets required a heavier weight of bombs from each B-26, resulting in a brace of the largest size weapons (the 1000-lb bomb) the aircraft could carry being expended. Two of these are seen falling away from their former 'hosts' in early 1944 (*Jim Crow*)

As Marauder missions piled up, so records began to be made. Long used to seeing pictures and stories about multiple-mission B-17s, the tactical flyers delighted in showing off their records in similar fashion through the historical medium of the painted bomb log. Among the first Marauders to fly 50 missions was 41-31877 *Bar Fly* (coded RU-V) of the 554th BS/386th BG (*USAF*)

It's human nature to disparage an object held in high esteem, and *Privy-Donna*, alias B-26B 41-31658/RU-A of the 454th BS, was a perfect case in point – the pilot of this bomber, which completed over 100 missions, was Capt E E Curran. It is seen here being worked on at its Boxsted hardstand between sorties in early 1944, the bomber displaying interesting details including the whip aerial forward of the windshield, the D/F (direction finding) loop 'bullet' aft of the nosewheel doors and the open escape hatch for the pilot (*USAF*)

tail gunner. Everyone on our crew is also a gunner. We have 11 .50 in Browning machine-guns.

'With everything checked we climb into the plane and dress. This is one big job for we will (later) have a temperature of -20 degrees and colder. I have on, when fully dressed, two pairs of long johns, army pants and shirt, gabardine flying coveralls, sheepskin coat and pants, life-vest, parachute harness and throat mike. I can hardly move.

'I'm a radio-op/gunner, but on this mission I'll be nothing but a gunner unless we fall out of formation. Then I will take over the radio. The lead radio operator does it all for the formation.

'My pilot has checked everything to his satisfaction. We taxy out for the take-off. Cleared at last, we trundle out onto the runway. We listen as those great Pratt & Whitneys thunder into life. We move very slowly at first. Then the props seem to grab air and we accelerate very rapidly. One hundred and thirty mph and we have lift. This is the critical time. To lose an engine now would indeed be very bad. Our plane is performing perfectly. (Thank God – one more time). Pilot tucks in the wheels and we are flying beautifully. We circle the field once and head for Europe.

'Each man alone with his thoughts now. No talking. The 23rd psalm is my standby. I while away the very cold and extremely noisy miles with that beautiful thought, "Yea though I walk through the valley of the shadow – we will soon be in the shadow".

'We are approaching land now. We will go in south of Amsterdam, circle north and bomb on the way out to sea. No sign of life, except the 14 beautiful Spitfires. They're Polish, from No 11 Group. None better. Once I saw a Spit take a direct hit. As it was falling I thought of the scripture, "Even for a friend, one might lay down his life". I never knew him, but he was my friend.

'Here is the bomb run. Must be straight and level for the bombardier. The Germans know this – and here comes the flak . . . very intense . . . very accurate.

'When you can hear explosions behind two 2000 hp Pratt & Whitneys, it's too close. It moans, it roars, it sputters. I see fire between me and the next plane. We are flying through a German flak box, a mathematical measurement of planned shooting that, in theory, even a bumble bee cannot get through.

'"Bombs away!"

'The plane leaps with the release of those blockbusters. Close the doors and dive. We are leaving in a

Getting the 'low-down' on loading, an armourer advises while one of the Marauder's aircrew gunners appears to be doing all the heavy work at the 554th BS dispersal at Great Dunmow. The machine in the foreground has red-outlined national insignia, whilst the B-26B-15 in the background is 41-31621 (*USAF*)

hurry. I watch the bombs making their run along the target. Looking back from 50 miles out to sea, I can still see the smoke from those guns.

'Our bomber is flying beautifully, thank God, and we come home in record time. Empty bombers fly like fighters. My pilot puts us down smoothly and we are happy. No "meat wagon" awaits us as it did on my second mission. My tail gunner received the Silver Star for that mission – three wounded men aboard, fires, flat tyres to land on – but that's another story.

'Debriefing first thing. Intelligence wants to know everything. Then we unload our heavy gear, pick up our valuables, head for the mess, then the sack. We are all in – dead tired, anoxia, lack of oxygen. We will rest, for we might be called upon soon. Once I flew two missions one day and more the next.

'Our group has lost one plane. Six badly wounded men have been brought back. Forty planes have been hit by shrapnel and three crash landed. We suffer losses quietly. No funerals for flyers. Wrap up their belongings in a blanket and ship to the Orderly Room.

'I'm the oldest man in our barracks now, so I wait. If you like math, the laws of probability tell us that we will be dead at 39 missions. I passed that mark long ago. Just one more mission – cold, lonely, dangerous and very, very, selfish. Since none of our immediate squadron had been lost, we are happy. How awful is war!'

The intelligence report on this mission is as follows: 'Four groups participated and put up 216 aircraft for a maximum effort to devastate the airfield. The 322nd had one shot down and 34 of its 54 aircraft battle damaged, plus two crash landings; the 323rd lost *Raunchy Rascal* with Lt George F Pipher's crew over the target and had six men wounded and 40 B-26s hit by flak, of which three crash landed; the 386th lost *Hell's Fury* and Capt Sanford's crew from a direct hit, and had 35 damaged, with *Man O'War* so badly shot up that the pilot had to belly it in at Stansted depot. The 387th fared a little better with 38 damaged and no losses'.

Quite apart from flak and fighters, the most effective deterrent to good bombing results was Europe's notoriously changeable weather. American airmen fresh to the ETO soon came to understand the English obsession with the weather – one that they were reluctantly forced to emulate. Lousy weather meant scrubbed missions, and a longer combat tour until they were completed.

To overcome the problem of cloud obscuring targets from bombardiers using conventional 'daylight' sights, the force was boosted during December by the availability of the British blind bombing aid 'Oboe'. Mk II sets were fitted in B-26s, and the 322nd BG's Maj Robert A Porter was selected to form a special unit with aircraft so converted – this became the 1st Pathfinder Squadron (Provisional) on 16 February 1944.

'Oboe' was particularly suited for installation in the B-26, as the latter had a fuselage spacious enough to accommodate the necessary equipment in both the navigator's compartment and the rear bomb bay. Accurate enough (on average plus or minus 400 ft) over short ranges, 'Oboe' was all but impervious to jamming – it was superior in this respect to 'Gee', the navigational aid which had been in use for some time by lead B-26s.

During the autumn and winter of 1943/44 'Oboe' enabled 92 obscured targets to be attacked by the 'mediums'. When clearer conditions permitted aerial photography of 75 of those targets, it was found that bombs had found their mark on 71 of them. From this analysis, Ninth Air Force made an educated assumption that the rest had similarly

It could be back-breaking work loading scores of bombers between a seemingly ceaseless series of missions, and the groundmen were grateful for simple, but effective, help. The American bomb truck, complete with angle-iron racks and girders, enabled crews to slide the ordnance off onto dollies, which were then hauled under the open bays. The B-26B providing the backdrop for this atmospheric shot was nicknamed *EXTRA ?* – note its impressive bomb log (*T Bivens*)

been hit. Bombing on instruments therefore became an integral part of B-26 operations for the remainder of the war.

Actual medium bombing results were assessed and graded by the AAF in four categories: 'superior' meant that all bombs had fallen with an imaginary 250-ft circle drawn around the centre of the target, the DMPI (Direct Main Point of Impact), whilst 'excellent' was all bombs within a 500-ft circle. An 'Unsatisfactory' assessment meant that most of the bombs had missed the target, or that only ten per cent had hit. The final category was 'undetermined', and as its title suggests, this was the most difficult to assess as it indicated that a target was quickly obscured from both human view and the lenses of aerial cameras – usually by smoke from the first bombs dropped. Alternatively, cloud or mist could be a factor in an undetermined classification.

Such results were frustrating for the crews, as the target in question would most likely be scheduled for a repeat raid. Nevertheless, the confidence the Ninth had in the Marauder was emphasised by the fact that no other AAF formation used a bombing classification higher than excellent. That all B-26 groups were capable of achieving superior results was gratifying to the crews, group commanders and higher command echelons.

In January 1944 an event of no small significance took place – a B-26 of the 322nd BG flew its 50th mission. Considering that six months previously most people would have viewed such an event as something dreamt up by a Hollywood scriptwriter, the fact that B-26B-25 41-31819, nicknamed *MILD AND BITTER* after the well-known British beer, had reached this figure was cause for celebration at Great Saling. And the air and groundcrews made the most of it.

Other Marauders, not to mention individual aircrew members, were also approaching the 'magic 50' mark. At around this time it was also decided that 50 missions would henceforth represent a tour for flight-crews in B-26 squadrons.

During January and February the B-26 groups settled into a pattern of flying bombing missions on a virtual daily basis, and adding two or three morning and afternoon sorties on certain days, weather permitting. *Noball* targets were heavily attacked, the 322nd interspersing these with more standard fare, particularly airfields – these included Gilze-Rijen, Deelen and St Trond.

There was a great variety of targets to be neutralised before the invasion, and in order to prevent the Germans getting the slightest hint of the actual location the Allies had selected to come ashore, the entire north-east coast of continental Europe had to be pounded. This policy successfully denied the Germans hundreds of miles of the French, Belgian and Dutch railway network, plus road and river links to the Channel coast.

Most Luftwaffe airfields within striking range of Normandy were ren-

The yellow and black striped tail band carried by B-26s of the 387th BG was arguably the most distinctive, and therefore effective, tactical recognition marking used by Marauder groups assigned to the Ninth Air Force. The code letters KX identify this bomber as belonging to the 558th BS (*Phil Jarrett*)

dered virtually untenable. German air commanders now found it all but impossible to operate without suffering significant losses in aircraft, personnel and facilities. Many found it prudent to pull back out of range of the twin-engined bombers. This part of the Ninth's campaign was at last bearing fruit after many months of hard work.

Although predominantly an Eighth Air Force strategic campaign, the period between 20-25 February 1944 – known as 'Big Week' – also involved the 'mediums' of the Ninth, who were charged with maintaining pressure on the Luftwaffe fighter force by continually bombing their airfields. Both the 322nd and 323rd BGs distinguished themselves during this period, crews from the former unit being cited for their achievements through the eventual awarding of a DUC.

On 15 February Col Gerald E Williams' 391st BG, based at Matching, became the first of the second group of B-26 units assigned to the Ninth to go operational. With its 572nd, 573rd, 574th and 575th BSs, the group adopted the identification marking of a yellow equilateral triangle on the fin-rudder of its aircraft in line with current Allied policy. All markings were based on two colours, with yellow and white being used for horizontal and diagonal stripes and triangles. The exception to this rule was the 322nd, which was identified by not bearing any distinguishing tail markings.

After an initial diversionary mission on 29 February, the 344th BG (494th, 495th, 496th and 497th BSs) went operational on 6 March, led from Stansted by group commander, Col Reginald F Vance. The target that day was Bernay St Martin aerodrome, which the 344th duly bombed. The crews experienced their first flak, and four aircraft came home with a few holes. The following day it hit the airfield at Conches, the 344th's bombing being rated as 'very good' by Command, which duly prompted a message of congratulations from 99th CBW headquarters.

On 8 March the 344th sent 54 Marauders to Soesterburg. The weather over England was cloudy, and in the poor visibility two B-26s collided, carrying all six men in each crew to their deaths. The rest pressed on, and again the bombing was praised.

The 394th BG (584th, 585th, 586th and 587th BSs) flew its first mission from Boreham on 23 March, Col Thomas B Hall commanding. Several theatre training sorties and one diversionary mission had been flown prior to the real thing, the crews being surprised at not being granted a 30-

day training period before their first combat mission. This was undoubtedly due to the closeness of the invasion, although of course nobody was aware of the date of D-Day.

Despite good navigation to Beaumont-le-Roger aerodrome, the 394th bombed long through cloud cover. Better results would be achieved three days later, when the Marauders returned to Imjuiden. As the target that had humiliated the men of the 322nd BG, and almost wrecked the B-26's chance of becoming an effective 'medium', Imjuiden was a 'natural' for a return visit. The opportunity was taken on 26 March. As a sea-bordered conurbation, the Dutch town held, apart from a power station, a number of other industrial installations including those supporting E-boats.

Pens for the latter were the primary targets for the Marauder bombardiers that day, who counted among their number men of the 394th. For them this was their real debut mission, and a tough baptism it proved to be. Laying on a 'maximum effort' force of 52 Marauders, the 98th CBW lost one aircraft to the flak defences and had numerous others suffer varying degrees of damage.

A positive demonstration of the B-26's new effectiveness was the fact that the 322nd (dubbed 'Nye's Annihilators') led the entire force, which totalled some 344 aircraft. The 322nd's contribution was 54 Marauders, all of which returned home, albeit with 20 of them having been holed by exploding flak shells. About 100 tons of bombs fell on the base and the crews counted at least four direct hits. 17 May 1943 had been avenged.

That flak could be effective in shielding targets without destroying bombers was demonstrated on the 394th's tenth mission on 12 April. Out after German rail guns at Dunkirk, the group flew an experimental pathfinder mission using 'Oboe'. This necessitated a long, straight, course, and on this occasion conditions were clear. This theoretically gave the flak gunners ample time to range in their weapons while the Marauders were still halfway across the Channel, and indeed the crews saw the deadly black bursts reaching out for them all the way into the target and out. Despite this attention, only superficial damage was caused to the aircraft – on the other hand, all the bombs fell wide of the target.

On 9 May, *MILD AND BITTER* did it again by becoming the first B-26 to complete 100 missions from England. Great Saling went wild as the Marauder touched down after bombing Evreaux/Fauville airfield, near Rouen, that afternoon. At the controls for the 29th time was Paul Shannon, who had first flown this particular ship on 12 August 1943. Ninth Air Force publicity was not slow to milk this success for all it was worth, and Shannon was called upon to do his bit;

'All the flak missed us by a safe margin. *MILD AND BITTER* has often been called the "luckiest ship in the Ninth Air Force", having collected less than 50 flak holes, most of them small ones. Only once has battle damage kept her on the ground – a few days ago, when

First with 50 up! The famed *Mild and Bitter* of the 452nd BS was held in great esteem around the dispersals at Great Saling, the aircraft (flown at the time by Paul Shannon) going on to complete more than 100 missions. Eventually sent back to the US, the B-26 was written off before it could be preserved for posterity – that honour instead fell to its great 449th BS rival *Flak Bait* (USAF)

33

repairs on an electric line required about four hours, which wasn't enough time between missions.

'Her engines are the same ones that first were installed. Only a magneto change, a hydraulic pump change and a few routine spark plug changes have been made. She has never made a one-engine return and never aborted a mission because of mechanical failure.

'In her 100-mission career, *MILD AND BITTER* has flown 449

Top Sarge of the 387th BG came to grief in England at the end of a rough mission. The cushioning effect of the B-26's low-slung engines (and four-bladed props) often meant that a 'straight in' belly landing resulted in a repairable aircraft, rather than a write off. In evidence at the wing root of '704 is a single horizontal 'stall strip', which reputedly broke up the airflow over the inner wing area sufficiently enough for the pilot to retain some semblance of control for a while longer when the aircraft was throttled back – crucial for an aircraft like the B-26, which possessed such a high stalling speed (*Crow*)

hours and 30 minutes, 310 hours and 40 minutes of that in combat. She has travelled approximately 58,000 miles – more than twice around the world – and burned some 87,790 gallons of gasoline. She has carried 166 crewmen into battle, yet never has a casualty been suffered aboard her.'

Shannon rounded out the glowing testimonial by giving a few details of the old ship's combat achievements;

'Altogether she has hit military objectives in northern France 44 times, airfields 38 times (and) railway yards 14 times.'

Runner up for the first 100th mission accolade was another 322nd BG aircraft, B-26B-25 41-31773 – the aptly-named *FLAK BAIT*, which would go on to even greater achievement. Strangely '773 was not held in such high esteem as '819, although competition to reach the 100 mark first was keen. Part of the reason was that *FLAK BAIT* more than lived up to her name, for she collected the stuff like the proverbial magnet. *MILD AND BITTER*, incidentally christened by her Texan crew chief William Stuart only after the ship had flown about 40 missions, was definitely the all-round favourite. Nobody really knew why.

From 15 May airfield attacks were confined to those situated within a 130-mile radius of Caen. This was designed to push the Luftwaffe back at least as far as Allied aircraft would have to fly to reach the invasion beaches. The overall plan was to completely isolate Normandy and Brittany by destroying the main river bridges. This would compel the enemy to unload supplies and troops, ferry them across rivers by pontoon or boats, and reload them onto trains on the other side of the waterway. All this would take an inordinate amount of time. And the Allied air forces had no intention of allowing the Germans to then proceed unmolested – backed-up locomotives and rail freight wagons would be ceaselessly bombed and strafed, as would river traffic. When he finally had no choice but to take to the roads, these too would be heavily interdicted.

STRAIGHT EIGHT

With Col Richard T Coiner at the helm, the 397th BG (566th, 597th, 598th and 599th BS) went operational from Rivenhall on 20 April. It was the eighth, and last, of the Ninth Air Force's Marauder units to see action. A debut combat mission to bomb a seemingly innocuous French field at a place called Le Plouy Ferme may have seemed odd to the crews, but it harboured a V1 'nest'.

The 397th came to England with an outstanding Stateside training record 'never before equalled', and a trophy to prove it. Group crews flew about 75 camouflaged B-26B-55s to England, many of which had been fully or partially stripped back to natural metal finish by D-Day.

On 27 April the 394th unwittingly experienced one of the ironies of war. The Marauders carried out an excellent pattern bombing of the marshalling yards at Cambrai and thought little more of it until later when the 'Bridge Busters' moved to France to be stationed just outside the city. The Americans were entertained by the local mayor, who was delighted that the B-26s had been so careful in placing their bombs.

With the invasion looming, the pace of operations quickened considerably during May. Tactical air forces were given five major groups of target which had preferably to be neutralised before Operation *Overlord* began – coastal gun batteries, rail communications, bridges over the Seine, bridges over the Meuse and airfields in France. The bridge campaign was opened on the 7th by fighter-bombers, the 'mediums' making their debut two days later when B-26s hit the Meuse crossings. A high degree of accuracy was required, and Marauder bombardiers were carefully briefed in order to reduce the risk of bombs falling short or long.

The 397th experienced a deadly flak barrage on 28 May when it was briefed to bomb the Maissons Lafitte rail bridge across the Seine. No Marauders were lost, and although 21 returned with holes, none were as large as that made in their target – the south span of the bridge was lying in the river by the time the B-26s turned for home.

It was a different story for the 344th. Its target on the 28th was Mantes-Gassicourt railway bridge, this follow-up strike just 24 hours after they had initially hit it being staged in an effort to prevent the inevitable repairs that were quickly put in hand by the Germans. Although 36 bombers were on the mission, only 19 were able to bomb accurately and five were shot down either in the immediate area, or later as a result of damage received. Near-miss explosions of shells also created enough turbulence to throw some of the bombardiers off their aim.

Despite these difficulties, B-26 groups became increasingly adept at placing their high explosive bombs in relatively small areas with good concentration. Command had determined from statistical analysis that it took six B-26s bombing as one some 150 sorties to obtain a single direct hit on a bridge. This figure was deemed economical enough, and in fact was reduced to a direct-hit-per-sortie ratio of 92 on a series of missions to destroy nine rail and thirteen road bridges between Paris and the coast before the invasion.

For the crews, this higher echelon confidence in them reflected in excellent morale. The men who flew Marauders were now well and truly 'in the groove'. They regarded their aircraft as one of the best in the AAF inventory, and there was definitely an extra 'buzz' – even a mystique – in flying an aircraft lesser mortals thought of as dangerous and difficult to handle. Those in the know enjoyed scotching such loose talk, and nobody concerned with Ninth Air Force tactical operations minded pilots going around telling people that you had to be good to fly a B-26.

Martin's development programme continued to improve the Marauder, no modification being as significant as the 3.5° change in wing incidence. Designed to reduce the take-off and landing run, improve propeller clearance when the aircraft was on the ground and enhance visibil-

Boasting a finely-detailed Indian chief on its nose, this 584th BS/394th BG B-26B was appropriately nicknamed *Ish-Tak-Ha-Ba*, which meant 'sleepy eye' in Indian parlance. It was also the name of a town in Minnesota where the original pilot of the Marauder – Lt Martin Harter – hailed from. As well as the striking nose art, the aircraft also had a second skilfully-rendered Indian portrait painted on the nosewheel cover. Its bomb log tally eventually denoted over 100 sorties (*Crow*)

ity from the flightdeck, the new wing configuration was introduced on the B-26F-1 during the spring and summer of 1944.

With the last B-26C-45 completed in April 1944, the Omaha plant ended Marauder production in favour of the B-29. Martin had by that time built 300 B-26Fs and gone onto the B-26G, which proved to be the final combat model. How well it compared to earlier Marauders was highlighted by the then Lt Col Franklin S Allen, Jr, who had not only served as a highly experienced test pilot, but also as a B-26 skipper both in the Pacific and with the 386th BG in Europe. Allen was quoted in a Ninth Air Force press release concerning the B-26G, which was first delivered to depots in the ETO in July;

'It's a far cry from my first B-26, which I flew in the south-west Pacific, to the G-model I'm now flying in the ETO. I find the stepped-up performance of the G, with its new emergency landing gear and improved gasoline system, far superior to other models. Many of our B-26s have been saved by use of these improved features. Many that were lost would have been saved if they had had them.'

Commenting on the merits of the 'tipped' wing, Allen reported;

'At first I didn't like the change, but I soon found that it affords much wider visibility – and makes it easier to pick up the target, when every second counts. You are able to see a lot more out of the B-26 now, because the large nose no longer obstructs the view.'

Among other features of the B-26G was the deletion of the fixed gun in the lower starboard side of the nose and removal of the useless torpedo fittings – maximum bomb load remained at 4000 lbs, however.

Ammunition for all remaining machine guns was also raised to a total of 4400 rounds. The package guns were retained, although they occasionally gave trouble through faulty ammunition feeds and jammed rounds. Although they were not required on numerous missions, the packages themselves were generally retained on Ninth AAF Marauders, and some aircraft flew with the guns removed to save weight.

RAF fighter protection, which had been a necessary pre-requisite for Marauder operations in 1943, was gradually relaxed as the number of B-26s increased and the Luftwaffe was forced to all but abandon its forward bases. In any event it was realised that the German high command preferred to reserve its day fighters for the greater threat, namely US heavy bombers – a decision which rested very well with the Marauder men!

Escorts – which were now usually USAAF P-47s and P-38s – were provided as necessary, although flak, rather than German fighters, remained the greatest hazard to medium bomber operations. This was a primary factor taken to heart by Gen Anderson, who initiated a far reaching programme to improve the performance of the Marauders, and their crews. 'How far', he asked the men, 'did flak effect personal and crew performance in the target area?'

Anderson wanted honest answers to this, and dozens of other question. He realised that hauling bombs across the Channel was a pointless exercise if the targets could not be hit accurately. That he got what he wanted was reflected in the steady improvement in the B-26 force's bombing accuracy. Anderson also stressed maintaining crew integrity, and did not hesitate to bring new pilots, bombardiers and navigators into his groups if he felt changes were justified.

D-DAY TO THE ARDENNES

On 6 June, the Ninth Air Force's Ninth Bombardment Division undertook a series of missions that were demanding and potentially dangerous to the troops pouring ashore on the invasion beaches. Gen Anderson had undertaken to put 320 bombers over seven targets on 'Utah' Beach between H-Hour minus 30 minutes, and if necessary bring this down to minus half a minute. Needless to say, Anderson could not have taken this decision had he not had complete faith in his B-26 and A-20 crews' ability to do the job. What it essentially meant was that Allied troops would be running into the smoke generated by exploding bombs just a few hundred yards ahead of them. Attention to detail extended to the fact that if large bombs were used, those that missed their targets would make craters in the ground over which the invading soldiers would soon be traversing – and nothing was allowed to impede their progress.

Beginning at 0517 on 6 June, single squadrons of B-26s began flying a relay system of strikes on specific targets. Their bomb bays were loaded with 100-pounders fitted with instantaneous fuses. Timing was vital, and

There were so many ships in the Channel on 6 June that pilots quipped 'you could almost walk across from England, stepping from one to another'. Getting a grandstand view of proceedings, the crews of a full combat box of eight 555th BS B-26s are seen flying their second or third mission of the day. In the lead is 41-31812, nicknamed *Mr Five by Five*, which had completed 75 missions by July 1944. Marauders were among the first aircraft over the beaches on that momentous morning
(*USAF via M Bowman*)

crews were told to bring their bombs home if there was the slightest suspicion that they had missed their slot to release.

It was soon realised that the normal Marauder box formation of 18 aircraft was too big for the precision required on the first morning of *Overlord* – the box size was reduced to six. This meant that if a target was missed when the lead bombardier gave the signal, less ordnance would fall among friendly troops.

In company with dozens of other tactical aircraft flying out across the Channel, Marauders of the 394th BG's 586th BS get underway for another June 1944 mission. Few invasion-period sorties could be termed 'milk runs', although many were of short duration, enabling aircrews to complete their stipulated 50-mission tours relatively quickly. Many individuals chose to stay on and fly more, however (*Crow*)

Initially, the 'mediums' were to bomb visually from a minimum altitude of 4000 ft, but when the latest weather forecasts for D-Day were to hand, this bombing height was reduced to below 3500 ft. Conditions were still far from ideal when the decision to go was made. Take-off was set for between 0343 and 0500. The weather was foul, with persistent rain and an overcast, and crews were doubtful. Would they ever to able to form up correctly? Would they even see their targets in this stuff?

Eventually, some 400 Marauders did take-off to arrive over the beaches on time. The first objective was three coastal gun batteries immediately in front of the British assault area. At 0605 B-26s were over 'Utah' Beach, and 20 minutes later bomb bays were opened over a further five batteries, which quickly became a lesser threat to American troops pinned down on 'Omaha' Beach. Some crews found they were bombing from 4000 ft while others dropped as low as 2000 ft – the weather refused to stay put.

Flying parallel to the beaches, the bombers released their loads and then flew back to base to be bombed up and refuelled ready for the next sortie. Crews were then quickly debriefed, before heading back to Normandy again. Nobody wanted to miss this show, and some aircraft took off with only half their crews aboard, the necessary duties being shared between those who were available.

One of the hundreds of Marauder crewmen over the beaches on D-Day was bombardier Charles Middleton of the 496th BS/344th BG. He recalls that historic day;

'At 0100 hours on the 6th I was sleeping soundly, only to be aroused by the GQ at about 0130 for the morning briefing. I haven't the slightest

This dispersal scene at Great Dunmow in June 1944 shows a B-26F of the 553rd BS being readied for yet another invasion support mission. During the early weeks of Operation *Overlord*, tactical bombers flew multiple cross-Channel missions on a daily basis, and in order to minimise their time on the ground re-arming, B-26s were bombed up with ordnance pre-stacked at dispersals by squadron armourers (*USAF*)

idea what I had for breakfast. As for clothing, I wore what I usually did to fly a combat sortie – a uniform shirt and trousers over my pyjamas and a flight suit over the uniform, plus an A-2 jacket. I wore my billed, "50-mission crush" hat because a flak helmet fitted over it. I had on my brown riding boots which wouldn't come off if we had to bail out – and my fleece-lined flying boots which fitted better than with the GI boot.

'In-flight clothing of a sort was added – a Mae West and a parachute harness. I kept my chest pack on the radio operator's table. Over all this went a flak jacket, usually donned when nearing France.

'The mission briefing took place at 0230 hours. One of the main points I vividly recall was the number of German aircraft that could be brought against us, but not to worry – there would be 7000 Allied airplanes in the air!

'The weather was ghastly: low clouds, drizzle and fog. As I recall, we took off about 1400 hours. The attempt to join up in proper formation was a mess. We missed the main formation and chased the group halfway across the Channel; as the sky brightened we caught up with them and took a position that looked empty. I thought then, and still do, that I was in the 13th Marauder to cross the "Utah" beach-head, regardless of mission logs, group histories and that sort of thing. The 344th had been selected to lead all the other groups, so we were the first.

'Crossing the Channel, it looked to me as if you could walk ship to ship without getting your feet wet. As we neared the coast we could see naval gunfire and some return fire. We were scheduled to be over the beach before the troops came ashore, at about 0630 hours.

'Because of the low cloud deck, our bombing altitude was low at about 3500 ft. We flew parallel to the shore line and dropped our 250-lb bombs directly on the beach, in the sand. I thought to myself that we were digging foxholes and exploding mines.

'As far as we were concerned, it was a milk run. The return to Stansted, three hours and fifty minutes later, was uneventful. Thus ended my thirtieth combat sortie.'

Middleton went on to make it 67 sorties and 230 hours of combat time before finishing his tour on 11 September 1944.

Allied air superiority made it possible for the medium bombers to fly their missions without fear of molestation by Luftwaffe fighters, resulting in them literally parading up and down the beach areas almost as though they were on a bombing range. Even German ground fire was well contained, and the cost of the day's operation was just three B-26s and fifteen crewmen.

By the end of the 'Longest Day' the B-26s and A-20s had contributed over 1000 sorties to the 4656 flown by all elements of the Ninth Air Force in support of the greatest invasion in history. What the early morning bombing had achieved was difficult, if not impossible, to assess. In the words of the

Taking the 'high road' to the battle front on 12 June, these Marauders of the 587th BS/394th BG were actually flying south-west of Paris when the anonymous photographer snapped them. In the foreground is one of many B-26s that had its AEAF 'stripes' correctly applied ('broken') as per instructions, thus allowing the code (in this case 5W-M) to remain legible – the letters often failed to show up particularly well against olive drab paint, at least in wartime photographs! (*Crow*)

Invasion support sorties inevitably took a steady toll on the Marauder ranks as German ground fire seemed ever-present, despite the deluge of high explosive – much of it dropped by B-26s. On 23 June *Blazing Heat* of the 386th BG suffered a nose-over at Great Dunmow, and having completed over 90 missions up to this point in its frontline career, the B-26 was saved from the scrap heap as neither its air- or groundcrew wished to see one of the 398th's veterans junked. '585 was duly repaired, and it went on to complete its century (*USAF*)

After picking up no less than 264 holes from shrapnel on a mission over St Omer, this 397th BG B-26 was rather inevitably dubbed *Patches*. Few sections of the groundcrew on B-26 bases worked harder than the 'sheet metal men', who were constantly employed cutting, shaping and riveting new panels to the bombers' fuselage and wings in an effort to cover over the gashes made by German flak (*Crow*)

Their crews comforted by the presence of a couple of P-47s in the background, Marauders of the 394th fly over Connflannes on 12 June. These 'little friends' were usually successful in warding off German fighter attack, resulting in flak batteries being left to claim the vast majority of B-26s kills – on the day after this photograph was taken, the B-26B-55 in the foreground (42-96210/5W-P of the 587th BS) was shot down (*Crow*)

AAF official history, 'Where the effects of part of the "mediums"' effort on "Utah" Beach could be later followed, 35 per cent of the bombs were reported to have fallen to seaward of high water mark, but 43 per cent (were) within 300 ft of their target'.

In summary, the history noted that if the material results of the bombardment were not as great as was hoped, the positive morale effect on Allied troops – in equal measure to the detrimental effect on the Germans – was very valuable indeed. Of all the B-26 groups participating on D-Day none did as well as the 386th. Having the honour of going in last (when the landing forces would be nearest, and therefore most exposed, to their bombs), the group further enhanced its record as the best in the Ninth at that time. Their bombs fell just six-and-a-half minutes before the first troops came ashore.

In the days following the invasion, the 'mediums' were able to range out from the Normandy coast and help maintain the isolation of the bridgehead. On 7 and 8 June the 387th BG was congratulated for its sterling work in preventing the tanks of the 17th Panzer Division from reaching the invasion area. Having being informed that the divisison was moving north by rail, the B-26s tried unsuccessfully to bomb a junction at Rennes on the 7th, but some damage was done nevertheless to the railway west of Vire, causing a choke point of vehicles at St Lo. The following morning Pontabault junction was accurately bombed, whilst in the afternoon the group finally halted the panzers.

The latter mission proved to be one of the roughest, and most remarkable, ever flown by the group. Capt Rollin D Childress was to lead 18 aircraft against a fuel dump in the Foret de Grimbosq, south of Caen. Take-off was at 1958 hours into a weather ceiling of just 900 ft. The formation assembled without difficulty, but whilst climbing through the

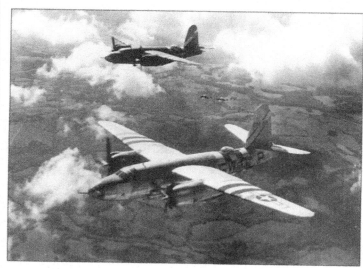

solid overcast aircraft became widely dispersed – so much so that 11 of them returned. One crash-landed at Gravesend, in Kent, and another piloted by 1Lt Raymond V Morin was lost while attempting to land at Friston, on the Channel coast, in zero ceiling weather.

Childress rallied three aircraft to his own and continued on, sometimes at deck level, in 'quarter of a mile' visibility. He managed to find the target, and his bombardier, 1Lt Wilson J Cushing, aimed the bombs with great accuracy from a height of 6000 ft. As the formation of four B-26s turned off the target, moderate,

but extremely accurate, flak caught the fourth aircraft in the formation, flown by Capt Charles W Schrober. It exploded in mid-air, and no parachutes were seen – among the missing crewmembers was the 387th's weather officer, Capt John D Root.

Braving atrocious weather, the remaining trio of Marauders sped for home to land at Stoney Cross at 2220 hours. Childress was congratulated on his tenacity and perseverance by both Col Millard Lewis, CO of the 98th CBW, and Lt Col Thomas H Seymour, the group commander.

The effectiveness of the bombing was later attested to by a telegram from the army, which confirmed that the forest fuel dump containing the immediate supply for the entire 17th Division had gone up in flames.

Luftwaffe activity over the invasion area was severely curtailed by the vast Allied air umbrella, although when Normandy was finally confirmed as the area chosen to come ashore, the Germans rushed in fighter units in a desperate attempt to disrupt operations. Little success was achieved, but on 8 June the Bf 109G-equipped II./ JG 53 managed an attack on the Marauders. Lt Herbert Rollwage of 5.*Staffel* shot down a B-26 at 1047 that morning to claim his 63rd victory. Having been awarded the *Rit-*

Soon after the invasion had proved to be a success, the Ninth directed its groups to remove, or cover, their prominent AEAF stripes, lest aircraft were seen from above by unfriendly eyes. This led to B-26s exhibiting a scruffy and patched appearance for months to follow. Typical post-D-Day finish is shown here on both camouflaged and 'natural metal' Marauders from the 454th BS/323rd BG (*USAF*)

Son of Satan was one of the longer-lived Marauders assigned to the 386th BG. Part of the 555th BS, B-26B-15 41-31613 was coded YA-Y, and assigned to Maj Sherman Beatty, the squadron CO. He led the group on many occasions, having the unit's publicity machine well focused on the exploits of this aircraft – things like having 'Ike' photographed in the pilot's seat helped make it the most famous B-26 in the entire group (*T Bivens*)

The personalising of aircraft was an American practice followed very enthusiastically in all Marauder squadrons, and it was common for the name to appear on both sides of the fuselage. The Yankee Guerilla, *alias B-26C-15 41-34946 of the 386th BG, was one so decorated, although the bomb log appeared only on the port side – again a more or less standard procedure. Crew members such as these air evacuation nurses would have been very welcome indeed aboard any aircraft in the outfit! (via R L Ward)*

Painters took the time to make sure that '946 could be recognised instantly on the flightline from either side. Ribald names (and dames!) boosted morale, and demonstrably showed crew affection for 'their' particular bomber. Machines were often identified by their names alone (via R L Ward)

terkreuz just two months before this action, Rollwage eventually became the most successful German pilot against four-engined bombers. A 'twin' such as the Marauder was a little unusual for him, although other Allied 'medium' types did figure in his overall score of 102 kills.

Numerous AAF group commanders 'led from the front' and the 387th's Tom Seymour was no exception. Having taken over the group when the previous skipper, Jack Caldwell, had been shot down on 13 April, Seymour was himself killed in July in a crash near Ongar after a local flight. The 387th's reins were then passed to Col Grover C Brown, a B-26 pilot who had risen to be Chief of Staff of the 98th CBW.

Brown, however, hankered after a field command, and when the leadership of the 387th fell vacant, he persuaded Anderson that he was the right man for the job. Up to that point in the war the group had achieved only an average combat record, and Brown believed that they were capable of much more. As the new skipper, he would address any problems, thus putting the 'tiger tails' firmly 'on the map'.

Despite the success of the first days of the invasion, the Germans hung on tenaciously to every yard of Normandy, and Allied progress was painfully slow in those first weeks. Helping to wear down the defenders to the point where they would have little choice but to surrender, or flee, the Ninth maintained an air umbrella over the front for days on end. Enemy strength was whittled down, with little or no opposition from the Luftwaffe, which could only manage isolated attacks on Allied ground forces. In the air, the 'mediums' were even less troubled by enemy fighters.

FORWARD AIRFIELD

With the invasion a reality, some of the first troops landed in Normandy were AAF personnel equipped with tools, not weapons. The men of Ninth Engineer Command were specialists who prepared forward airfields and landing strips for fighters, medium bombers and transports to give direct support to the armies. In some areas of France it was decided to bulldoze new airstrips rather than repair existing ones that had been occupied by the Luftwaffe. In many cases, the latter had been deliberately wrecked if the enemy had had the time, and booby traps, mines and snipers were amongst the hazards faced by the engineers as they went about their construction work.

Pre-invasion planning had included analysis of Normandy's

terrain, soil and drainage to identify the best sites for airfields. An integral part of the build up for D-Day had included the construction of millions of feet of PSP (pierced-steel planking) prefabricated sections of steel matting for building runways, together with the necessary pre-positioning of heavy equipment to prepare the ground, including bulldozers, graders, gasoline shovels and scrapers.

Engineers laid standard 3600-ft or extended 5000-ft PSP runways, strips of at least 4500 ft in length being required at most B-26 bases. Ground reconnaissance parties moved up with the forward troops, and as soon as an area was declared safe, construction work began – usually on several airfields at a time. Known as 'clutches', these were built as close to the frontline as possible. No fewer than 241 airfields between Normandy and Austria were prepared by war's end.

More than a few of the established French airfields had been damaged by American bombs, but at least the AAF was able to derive more advantage from their advance bases than the Luftwaffe had been able to in the months preceding D-Day. But there were times when it was more prudent to head back across the Channel, despite the existence of emergency strips in the beach-head area, as gunner George Cheadle of the 554th BS recalled at the time – his crew was on their 66th mission on 15 June, flying B-26B-15 41-31622, nicknamed *Litljo*, against targets in the St Lo area, and their aircraft had taken hits from heavy flak;

'I was in the top turret and saw a burst of flak just below and to the left of the cockpit. The explosion shook the airplane, and I saw smoke coming from the right engine. The pilot, Capt Asa Hillis, notified the crew that we had damage, and ordered the tail gunner and me to come forward to assist. Leaving the turret, I put on my chest pack parachute and started forward. I was unable to get through the bomb bay with the chest pack on, so I unhooked it and dropped it onto the floor of the plane.

'When I arrived at the cockpit I found that Capt Hillis had a piece of flak sticking out of his left wrist, but he was still flying the plane. I pulled the fragment, which had passed almost all the way through, out of his wrist. The radio gunner, Sgt Henry "Fireball" Farwell was in the nose serving as toggleer. He had head and lower body injuries and was covered with blood, but managed to crawl back to the radio room. The tail gunner, Sgt E J 'Mac' McDonnell, and I applied first aid.

'Captain Hillis had feathered the right propeller, and we discovered

The *'Guerilla* on a sortie during the early D-Day support period. The port engine appears to be named *EVE*, and undoubtedly the starboard Pratt & Whitney was similarly personalised. Such identities would occasionally be used on intercom talk, depending on the way familiarity of the crew (*via R L Ward*)

Making a beautiful portrait despite its grim task, B-26B-55 42-6131, coded YA-V and named *Perkatory II*, of the 555th BS/386th BG releases its deadly load of HE. Robert L Perkins was the ship's regular pilot, but he was shot down and made a prisoner in July 1944. He was not flying this aircraft at the time, however, the bomber serving as a replacement for *Perkatory*, which was lost in bizarre circumstances – a Ju 88A-14 of 8./KG 6 crashed on it (and two other B-26s) at Earls Colne in the early hours of 22 March 1944, having been shot down by a RAF Mosquito Mk XIII of No 488 Sqn. What made matters worse was that the 386th had only temporarily replaced the resident 323rd BG at the Essex base as part of a mobility exercise! (*T Bivens*)

Ninety plus, and counting. B-26 *Barbara Ann* of the 585th BS flew a further 35 missions after this one over France in mid-1944 to end up as one of the highest sortied Marauders in the 394th BG 'Bridge Busters' (*Crow*)

that the hydraulic system had been damaged in the nosewheel well. Hydraulic fumes were escaping into the cockpit and irritating our eyes. We had a small black dog on board and the fumes were making him bark and jump all over the radio compartment.

'The pilot, assisted by the co-pilot, Lt Jerry Soper, was able to head back to the coast and cross the Channel on one engine. We were told not to use the emergency strip on the beach-head since it was not safe for a single-engine landing. We landed at an RAF emergency metal strip at Friston on the coast. The nose wheel would not lock in the down position so Capt Hillis brought the Marauder in and held the nose high as long as possible, but when the nosewheel touched the runway, it collapsed. Amid a lot of dust, noise and sparks the plane wound up on its nose.

'Everyone got out, including the dog, who promptly ran away and we never saw him again. The pilot and radio-gunner were taken to the Oxford hospital in a small single-engine stretcher plane. The waist gunner was knocked unconscious during the landing, but everyone else got out without injury.'

Litljo had flown over 100 missions, but the damage sustained in the crash was too great to be economically repaired so it was scrapped. The Marauder's name came from a song – 'Little Joe the Rambler' – that the pilot used to sing over the intercom. This mission was the crew's last mission, for they went home to the States on R & R soon afterwards.

Instances of animals being carried in bombers were relatively few, but it was done, despite being strictly against regulations. The American penchant for pets of all kinds was renowned, and few bases were without at least a few dogs and cats. On occasion, crews sneaked their mascots aboard for operational flights, but Hugh Fletcher, bombardier of a 452nd BS Marauder named *Jezabelle*, went considerably further. The hound in question, glorying in the name 'Salvo', wore a specially-made parachute harness. When the 322nd BG flew training missions from Great Saling for crew members to practice emergency bail out procedures, 'Salvo' rode in the nose awaiting his turn.

The AAF's public relations machine did not shrink from writing up the story of this canine crew member who appeared to like making jumps. Photos were published showing 'Salvo' about to board the B-26 and when he had just landed with the aid of his small 'chute!

In order to put targets nearer to their Marauders, the 323rd, 387th and 394th flew to new airfields – Beaulieu, Stoney Cross and Holms-

ley South, respectively, all of which were in Hampshire – in July 1944. The 397th followed suit in August, moving to Hurn, in Dorset. These stations were occupied for just a few weeks, and acted as jumping off points for bases in France.

Pounding enemy positions in the St Lo area kept the 344th at Stansted occupied for the three days between 24 and 26 July. In that

time its aircraft hit troop concentrations, supply dumps, a railway viaduct and a bridge – a fine effort recognised by the award of a DUC. Citations for AAF groups and squadrons were awarded for meritorious service during single operations, for entire campaigns or, in the case of the 322nd BG, for a year of combat in the ETO. The latter award was announced on 24 July, and cited the period from 14 May 1943 to date. A week later a DUC was also presented to the 386th BG for a year's combat in Europe. Announced on 30 July 1944, it confirmed their record from that date in 1943. Such recognition reflected credit on all personnel from pilots and navigators to clerks and cooks – all were equally important to the smooth running of a combat group.

With its tail tip photographically cropped, B-26G-5 43-34409 hails from the rarely illustrated 451st BS of the 322nd BG. This shots accurately shows how the engines were canted up 3.5° on the B-26G (and F) when compared with earlier model Marauders. The 'twisted wing' B-26s were generally liked, although pilots would probably have stuck with the earlier, lighter, B- and C-models given the choice (*Crow*)

NIGHT FORAYS

Since the earliest days of the B-26's operational service it had been the intention to experiment with missions other than conventional day bombing, including night operations. Mindful perhaps that RAF night bombers did not generally attack tactical targets, resulting in a perceived nocturnal respite for German targets in France until American day bombers returned, an anonymous Pentagon official apparently gave the go-ahead for night bombing missions by Marauders.

Few Ninth Air Force officers showed much enthusiasm for their new task, but on the face of it, the decision had validity within a bigger proposal to have the Ninth operating 'round the clock'. If medium and attack bombers could bomb accurately at night, the support of troops in the field would be greatly enhanced. To this end, three groups (the 409th, 410th and 416th) that had equipped with A-20s in the early spring of 1944 were initially selected to concentrate on night attack missions, but a command decision substituted the 322nd in their place.

Night training commenced for the 322nd during April, and crews

B-26F-1 42-96313 of the 391st BG en route to a target during the summer of 1944. The code P2 denoted the 572nd BS (*Crow*)

immediately attempted to resolve the question of whether to operate in a stream, as practised by RAF Bomber Command, or as individual aircraft, with each crew navigating and dropping its bombs. In either case, it would be necessary to use Pathfinders dropping target markers. The effective night bombing altitude was established at between 4500 and 7000 ft.

Disaster could strike even before the enemy had fired a shot, as one Lt Fisher of the 556th BS found to his cost on 25 May 1944. Opening the throttles of *Lucky Lady* at Chipping Ongar, he was suddenly faced with total instrument failure. There was nothing for it but to scrub the mission and return to base, and Fisher might have pulled it off, but for another Marauder providing something of an obstacle just short of landing. '*Lady* clipped the tail of the second bomber and bellied in, causing considerable damage to herself in the process (*Crow*)

But once again Marauder crews were handed something that had not been thought through. The whole concept of using B-26s at night was vague, the aircraft were not modified for night work and had no exhaust flame dampers, whilst the crews pondered just how they were supposed to identify enemy fighters in the dark without any visual aids, and what they were supposed to do if they happened to be blinded by German search-lights in the target area. Their final question centred around how they were expected to fly a fully laden bomber back to England if the target could not be identified – few satisfactory answers were forthcoming.

Training nevertheless proceeded apace, with the 322nd's crews pro-gressively despatching more and more of their Marauders during the hours of darkness to flying loose formations of up to 54 aircraft before first light. Maintaining a safe separation distance was crucial, and this was set at at least 500 ft vertically and one minute horizontally. The 322nd's training lead was soon followed by all the other Ninth AF B-26 units, and although most were destined not to fly operationally at night, the 344th BG successfully assembled nocturnal formations of up to 36 aircraft.

One of a series of air-to-air photographs of 397th BG aircraft *Dee-Feater* taken by the incomparable Charles E Brown in July 1944 when he and writer Roger Montgomery visited the group at their Rivenhall base. The SHAEF-accredited correspondents published numerous photos and an article in the October issue of the British journal *Aeronautics* following their visit. Since then, Brown's colour and monotone shots of Lt Col Robert L McLeod's aircraft have appeared so frequently in publications that it is a strong contender for having become the most famous B-26 of them all! (*MAP*)

Finally, on the night of 23/24 May, the 322nd attacked Beaumont-le-Roger, led by two pathfinders. Few positive results could be determined from either this raid or a second mission staged a few nights later, but there were no losses through enemy action.

On the night of 7/8 July three 'Oboe'-equipped aircraft of the 1st PS(P) led the 322nd BG to attack the Chateau de Ribeaucourt in northern France. Identified by the Maquis as a headquarters for officers and technicians working on the V1 programme, this was a legitimate *Noball* target, but few realised the difficulties associated with destroying a single group of buildings in enemy territory at night. Barely trained for such work, crews would find the mission a challenge, to say the least.

In clear moonlight, the 322nd was soon being coned by groups of searchlights. Flak followed the Marauders, but worse still, the lights had attracted German nightfighters, and about ten miles into enemy territory, the night's carnage began. During the course of a reported 14 attacks, the enemy downed nine B-26s, whilst a survivor of the brief air battle was so badly battered (with 'over 1000 holes') that it limped back to Tangmere never to fly again. An 11th aircraft was badly damaged when its landing gear collapsed on touch-down. In total, 78 crewmen were missing.

Despite the opposition, the B-26s found the chateau and bombed on the pathfinder markers. Subsequently, it was found that all bombs fell 'near the target area, but about 150 yards from the principal buildings'. In all probability, the night flying Marauders were almost certainly a type the *Nachtjagd* had not previously encountered, and were thus incorrectly identified in their combat reports. And coincidentally the Bf 110 crews of NJG 6 claimed ten 'Wellingtons' destroyed on the night of 6/7 July, many months after that British twin-engined bomber had been withdrawn from such operations.

Assuming that the dates were merely confused by the German crews, it would have been logical at debriefing to identify an RAF aircraft that had frequently been intercepted over Germany when they were in fact the 322nd's B-26s. Even if they had been identified, claiming to have shot down B-26s would surely have caused raised eyebrows – everyone knew that Marauders were American day bombers which did not fly at night.

Heavy losses usually caused some searching questions, and after the 322nd's experience, the Americans themselves began having grave doubts about using the B-26 at night. It had been suggested that each of the Ninth's groups would fly night operations for one month rather than a set number of missions, and this was still on the cards when the 322nd flew its fourth on 4/5 August. Clear moonlit conditions again prevailed as the B-26s bombed fuel and ammunition stockpiled in the Foret de Fille. Only one enemy fighter was seen, plus some light and heavy flak, and two bombers were damaged.

Fuel supplies were also the target for the 322nd on its fifth night mission on 27/28 August. The location was Mont de Bolbec, and all but one of the 23 B-26s despatched released its load on pathfinder flares – all aircraft returned safely. Concurrently

Lt Col Robert McLeod with his aircraft when he was CO of the 596th BS. Named after his wife Dee, this B-26 acted as the lead ship on numerous missions during the summer of 1944. Incidentally, the 397th BG used the name 'Bridge Busters' as an unofficial title in mid-1944, as did the 394th. And the 397th's bare metal Marauders were quickly dubbed the 'Silver Streaks' by the press – a name also adopted by the 344th! Despite these descriptive sobriquets, all B-26 groups bombed bridges and operated silver aircraft (*Crow*)

A mixed flight of Marauders from the 391st BG includes P2-U from the 572nd BS and O8-B from the 575th. The latter aircraft (a B-26C-45) has either a replacement rudder fitted or the original item, which has yet to be stripped of paint. The other vertical marks on the rear fuselage appear to be masking strips for the AEAF stripes (*Hamlin via MacKay*)

Some Marauder nose art was elaborate and very well rendered – 'classy', as they might have called it in 1944. *Lucky Star* adorned the nose of group commander Col Thomas B Hall's B-26G-1 (43-34203), which was on the roster of the 584th BS/394th BG when based in France in 1944. The 68-mission bomb log was not allowed to compromise the artwork, and was thus relegated to the nosewheel door (*Crow*)

There was never was a contest for the 'scruffiest' Marauder of them all, but had there been, *Idiot's Delight* would have carried off the trophy. Certainly not alone in exhibiting a 'beat-up' appearance, B-26B-45 42-95808 of the 575th BS had served long and hard to become one of the veterans of the 391st (*Hamlin via MacKay*)

with the 322nd, the 323rd had also undertaken five night missions during August. Permission was granted for the participating aircraft to adopt a lower altitude than originally specified, and in the main, the white-tailed Marauders bombed from between 2500 to 3500 ft. Their first mission on the night of 6/7 August was to knock out a coastal gun battery at Ile de Cezembere, 41 B-26s being led in by five pathfinders. These aircraft bombed individually on target indicators.

Little news of what they achieved on night missions ever filtered back to the participating crews, most of whom felt the whole thing to have been a waste of time. It appears almost certain that very little was achieved, as after the 323rd attacked enemy targets on the nights of 9/10 August, further planned night missions by B-26 groups for three consecutive nights between the 12th and 15th were cancelled. Within a matter of days, the 323rd made ready to quit its temporary English home and shift to France as part of a general movement order that would ultimately see the Ninth's entire B-26 force based on the continent.

OPERATION COBRA

While fighter-bombers worked closely with ground forces, medium bombers had greater difficulty in striking accurately in areas lacking good visual reference points immediately forward of friendly troops. Operation *Cobra* – the breakout attack at St Lo in July – highlighted the problems bombardiers faced when 'mediums' and 'heavies' attempted to lay 'bomb carpets' on the enemy. On the opening day of the operation on 24 July, 580 Ninth AF 'mediums' were briefed to drop their loads in an area one mile deep and five miles wide. Unfortunately some bombs fell short and landed among troops of the US 30th Infantry Division.

Omar Bradley was asked by AAF commands to ensure that Allied troops were safely clear of falling bombs, and for the 'mediums', a minimum distance of 1450 yards was set. A distinct aiming point and split-second bomb release were obviously critically important.

Despite the accidents, *Cobra* was a resounding success. German forces were devastated, and on the 25th the US armies plunged forward to exploit the advantage, thrusting towards Avranches and then swing east to secure territory on the German flank. Desperate to save something from the shambles of the

The fetching nose art of *Idiot's Delight*, with part of the impressive bomb log that clearly showed that the aircraft had braved enemy defences over 100 times since joining its parent group

When the photographer got his angles just right, few bombers looked as impressive as the Marauder. Juggle the aperture a little and it even made the wing look longer! In reality, there was nothing wrong, in handling terms, with the 71-ft span wing on the mid to late production B-26s. An equally foreshortened angle could still make the wing look surprisingly small, however. These are aircraft from the 596th BS/397th BG

Normandy breakout, five Panzer divisions counter-attacked at Mortain – the weakest sector in the Allied line – on 7 August. For five days the battle raged, dominated totally by Allied airpower. In the end, the Germans-force was decimated, and the routed army began a headlong retreat towards the homeland via the Falaise-Argentan pocket – the graveyard of the Wehrmacht in France.

In an official AAF appraisal of air cover during the Normandy campaign, medium bombers were considered to be 'a mixed blessing'. While they were not as criticised as the occasionally errant 'heavies', (ground) commanders felt that they lacked the strong control and communication relationship with medium bomber units that they had with the fighter-bombers. '"Mediums" were also seen as too inflexible, lacking the quickness, ease of response and availability of the fighters'.

While there could be little denying that for direct battlefield support, fighter-bombers were more effective than 'mediums', the Marauder units' main strength lay further afield behind enemy lines. Regarding the effects of flak, this same AAF study noted that B-26s rarely flew low enough to take hits from small and light fire, but the heavier calibre weapons continued to take their toll.

Within the overall tactical war fought by the USAAF, air force chiefs identified a number of separate campaigns under which targets in a broadly-defined geographical area were attacked in a relatively small time frame for the duration of ground operations. It was during the northern France campaign, which officially began on 25 July 1944, that a B-26 pilot won his country's highest award for heroism.

By early August the Allies were well on the way to clearing all enemy forces from northern France, and the Marauder groups maintained the pressure on rear areas by knocking out the vital bridges that would enable enemy pockets to escape into Germany. During this phase, the 394th BG at Holmsley South chalked up its 100th mission of the war. Well living up to its 'Bridge Busters' nickname, the group had built for themselves a fine reputation by helping to wreck the French transportation system.

Focusing their efforts on the Loire region, Ninth Bomber Command sent the 'mediums' out on 1 August after bridges at Les Ponts de Ce and Cinq Mars and the embankment at Bouchemaine. Despite the B-26 being a relatively unusual type for members of the *Jadgwaffe* to attack, a number of *Jagdgeschwader* filed B-26 claims invariably for single aircraft during this phase of the war. One such claim for a Marauder shot down was made on 1 August by Uffz Alfred Reckhenrich of 15./JG 27 over La Meiganne, this being his premier victory in the Bf 109G. Understandably, such kills rarely identified the unit to which the bomber belonged, casting some doubt on the type of aircraft involved, rather than the claim.

On the morning of 7 August the

A crew eager to finish their duty in Europe and return to the 'good old US of A', and all the comforts of home, pose by B-26B-55 42-96191/9F-N of the 597th BS/397th BG – the two members of the groundcrew are lounging on a 1000-lb bomb. Many were dropped in anger by B-26s, whose crews would confirm that there was rarely any such thing as a 'milk run' in the ETO (*Hamlin via MacKay*)

Some aircraft names were unusual and made sense only to those in the know, such as the intriguing *QQQQ* on a B-26 of the 387th BG at St Dizier in 1944. The aircraft had flown at least 120 missions, and lacks the yellow segment of the group's tail marking – only the black stripes have been applied directly over the olive drab paint (*Crow*)

394th's target was again a bridge, this time at Nogent-sur-Seine. Attacking through accurate flak, the B-26s had lost three of their number before the bomb release point was reached, but the bridge was hit hard and the rail link severed. In the afternoon the 394th laid on a maximum effort, dropping 28 well-aimed tons of bombs on an ammunition dump at Bauches du Desert, south of Nantes. This was followed on the 8th by a mission to knock out a bridge over the Marne at Nanteuil. Splinters from heavy flak caused numerous crew injuries, and although 30 Marauders were damaged, none went down. One crewman did, however, bail out when he mistakenly thought his wildly-manoeuvring aircraft had been hit!

Two missions took place on 9 August, the railway bridge at Compiegne receiving highly accurate loads from the 394th – so much so that Brig Gen Harold L Mace (the new CO of the 98th CBW) sent a teletype describing the bombing as 'beautiful'. On the second misson of the day, Capt Darrell R Lindsey of the 585th BS led the group for the tenth time, 33 B-26s heading for the rail bridge across the river Oise at L'Isle Adam.

Despite their dire position, the retreating Germans hotly defended a number of fortified points against Allied air attack, and this particular bridge proved to be grimly typical in that respect. By the time Lindsey's aircraft approached the bomb release point, a number of his charges had been holed by exploding shells. As the formation came nearer, the Germans intensified their efforts to bring the bombers down.

Lindsey's own aircraft had already been holed, and suddenly the enemy gunners were right on target – the starboard engine took a direct hit. Blown out of formation, the crippled Marauder was skilfully brought back into the lead slot without disrupting the rest. Fire streamed back from the damaged engine, yet Lindsey, fully aware that the gas tanks could explode at any moment, continued on the bomb run. Not before the bombs went down in a good pattern did Darrell Lindsey order his crew to bail out. As the B-26 lost height, he held it steady so that eight crewmen could take to their parachutes. The bombardier was the last to leave. He offered to lower the wheels so that his pilot might have a chance to bail out. Lindsey, aware that this action could throw the Marauder into a spin, refused the offer. Reluctantly, the bombardier dropped through the open hatch.

As the crew drifted slowly down over enemy territory, they witnessed the final act of the drama. Fire reached the starboard wing fuel tank and it exploded. Wreathed in flames, the Marauder went into a terminal dive and crashed. For his determination and courage in leading the mission, Darrell Lindsey was subsequently awarded a posthumous Medal of Honor, which proved to be the only one to go to a B-26 crewman during the war. Of his crew, four men were made prisoner, three returned to the Allied lines and one was posted as missing.

In what had been a tough day for the 'Bridge Busters', 9 August also saw 2Lt Charles Kee's B-26 downed. Also from the 585th BS, Kee survived, as did other officers in his crew, but three enlisted men were lost.

In total, the 394th had flown five missions and lost five aircraft during the period 7-9 August, resulting in 37 men being posted MIA and six having returned seriously wounded. No less than 79 Marauders had been damaged by enemy action. For this effort, the 'Bridge Busters' were awarded a DUC, the accompanying citation for which praised both the air- and groundcrews – the latter in particular for their feverish, round-the-clock, repair work on damaged B-26s that ensured the group had the required number of bombers on the line for each mission.

While daylight operations occupied the Ninth's Marauders, night sorties by B-26s continued on a limited scale, those carried out in mid-1944 being of the 'special operations' nature. Such work was performed exclusively by the Eighth Air Force's 25th BG, based at Watton.

An example of their work was the night photography of *Noball* sites by the group's 654th BS who, whilst awaiting the delivery of Mosquito PR XVIs, used a handful of Marauders converted for this duty. Four new B-26Gs had been modified at Mount Farm – the Eighth's centre for PR activity – through the fitment of K-19B night cameras in the aft bomb bay in place of the ferry tank. Further extraneous equipment was removed to increase the bomber's speed, and a special olive drab and black finish was also applied to help mask the bomber's presence over enemy territory.

Operating under the codename *Dilly*, the 654th flew its first mission on the night of 10/11 August, followed by a further 13 (all performed by 43-34205, which had been the first B-26G modified) before the sites were captured by the Allies at the end of the month. Two other 25th BG Marauders flew three and four sorties respectively before *Dilly* was terminated – all four modified B-26Gs flew on as trainers until March 1945.

CLOSER TO THE ACTION

Shortening the distance the 'mediums' would have to fly to their targets could only improve their effectiveness, and in mid-August 1944 the 323rd, 387th, 394th and 397th BGs packed their bags and left for France. The 387th was declared operational again on 22 August at Maupertus (A-15), while the 394th occupied Tour-en-Bessin (A-13) and was ready to operate on 25 August. The 323rd was announced operational at Lessay (A-20) 24 hours later, whilst the 397th followed suit at Gorges (A-26) on the 30th.

A close up of the nose of B-26F-1 42-96290, featured on the previous page. This view clearly shows the additional applique armour plating fitted in order to better protect the pilot from flying shrapnel, as well as the twin aerial location points forward of the windshield. Salient details of the Plexiglas nose section, with its centreline .50 cal machinegun and associated bag for collecting empty shell cases, are also clearly visible (*Crow*)

Six days prior to commencing operations on the continent, the 394th had bombed the Foret de la Lande with 120 tons of 260-lb fragmentation bombs specifically to prevent German troops from crossing the Seine, near Rouen. Although it was not a clearly defined target, the enemy had been reported encamped in substantial numbers under the shelter of the trees, waiting to cross the river.

Having despatched 6602 sorties in August, Ninth Bomber Command now had five of its eight B-26s groups based in France, where they were better placed to blast French targets, including the port of Brest, in a series of missions beginning 5 September. The rest of the Ninth's Marauder units made ready to move to France during the second week of September, and by the 19th, the 391st BG was ready to fly missions from its new base at Roye/Amy (A-73). On 23 September the 322nd began operations flying from Beauvais/Tille (A-61).

On 25 September a designation change in the tactical command responsible for medium bomber operations took place to better reflect the expansion of the AAF in Europe; Ninth Bomber Command ceased to exist and Ninth Bombardment Division took over. A forward headquarters of the 98th CBW had previously been established at Lessay on 23 August, with that of the 99th being set up, also on 25 September, at Beaumont-sur-Oise (A-60). This was five days before the 344th BG began to fly continental sorties from the spartan surroundings of the airfield at Cormeilles-en-Vexin (A-59), the unit having left the comfort of Stansted behind. It was 2 October before the last of the UK-based Marauder groups made the move to France, the 386th bidding farewell to Great Dunmow and heading out across the Channel, also bound for Beaumont.

To their dismay, personnel of the 386th found they were now based at one of their former target airfields. The word was that a crater in the 555th BS area had been made by one of the group's own 1000-lb bombs, 'mediums' having done the job well at Beaumont – in the early days, the only habitable building became the operations office! And until GI ingenuity improved the place, the men were obliged to live in tents, a situation that prevailed through the bitter winter of 1944/45.

These base changes hardly brought a break in operations, the move cutting distances to targets by as much as 50 per cent for 'mediums'. Most of the groups quickly got used to a basic, nomadic, existence, and would eventually move deeper into Europe before the end of hostilities.

During October, rail bridges continued to dominate the long list of 'communications targets' drawn up for the medium groups, although missions were increasingly being flown only when the weather permitted. Along with the regular bomber sorties, Marauders also dropped leaflets on a few occasions, and although these exhortations to the enemy to surrender may have been largely ignored, any German soldiers who defected

Variations in paintwork were the rule rather than the exception on Ninth Air Force B-26s, as seen on 42-95964 – a B-50 of the 344th BG's 494th BS. Note how the old olive drab camouflage has been swept up towards the base of the fin, rather than running in a generally straight line, as was more the norm (*Crow*)

On Christmas Day 1944, just two days after the 397th BG had won a DUC for its work at the height of the Battle of the Bulge, a 596th BS pilot identified only by the surname of Colahan had to belly land B-26B-55 42-96204. This group was originally equipped with B-26B-55s, many boasting consecutive serial numbers

provided Allied Intelligence with valuable data, particularly on the effectiveness of tactical airpower.

A significant milestone was reached on 29 October when the 322nd BG chalked up its 300th sortie of the war with a strike on the Konz Karthaus railway bridge. This particular target had been briefed 'at least 15 times', and was to be etched in the memory of many Marauder men – particularly those flying with the 386th. The 387th moved to Clastres on 4 November, and unlike other B-26 groups, its aircraft would fly the remainder of their combat missions from this location.

Overcast conditions were having more of a disruptive effect on tactical operations than many veteran crews or planning staffs could ever remember – in this respect, England had been bad at times, but never like this! Aircraft remained grounded for days on end as the autumn deepened, but this did not prove to be too detrimental to the Allied war effort for commanders also noted a slackening of pace in the ground advance.

Some November days were clear, however, and therefore ideal for bombing. On the afternoon of the 26th, the 394th dropped a modest, but effective, 47 tons on a German supply depot at Bergzabern, the Marauder crews having earlier had to scrub the morning attempt to bomb the same target. The accuracy achieved on this sortie resulted in the group being awarded a commendation by the 98th CBW CO. Three days later the Ninth Bombardment Division was able to launch 3224 sorties.

Generally, however, forecasters could give air commanders few promises of long spells of good flying weather. December 1944 proceeded to demonstrate just how much poor weather could disrupt even the most powerful and well planned of air operations. Forward airfields became bleak, snowbound, wastelands, with living quarters a far cry from those the combat groups had enjoyed in England. Attempting to fly bombers laden with fuel and explosives in winter weather brought a spate of accidents when aircraft skidded off icy runways or taxyways and occasionally collided. When missions were able to get off, there was no guarantee that the target would be clear, or that it could be hit by anywhere near the same number of aircraft that had been 'on the board' to fly.

More often than not targets were found to be shrouded in mist or cloud. Aircraft frequently got lost, or had to return early with malfunctioning equipment – not uncommonly to a weather-related cause. It was a simple equation: if the Allied ground forces could not push into Germany, and if the air forces could not fly, the enemy could not be given the necessary *coup de grace* – short of a miracle, the war would most definitely not be 'over by Christmas'.

COLOUR PLATES

This 11-page section profiles at least one representative B-26 from each of the groups that saw combat with the Eighth and Ninth Air Forces between 1943 and 1945. The colour artwork has been specially-commissioned for this volume, and profile artist Tom Tullis and figure artist Mike Chappell

have gone to great pains to illustrate the aircraft, and their crews, as accurately as possible following in-depth research from original sources. B-26s that have never previously been seen in profile are featured alongside acccurate renditions of some of the more familiar Marauders of the period.

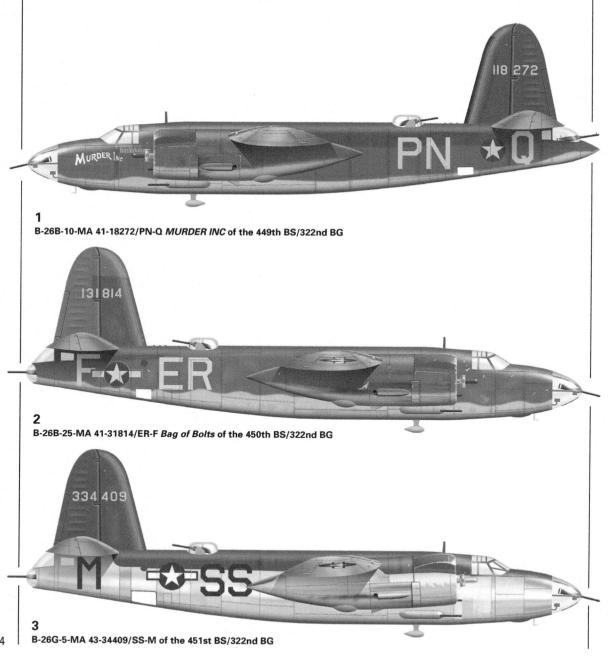

1
B-26B-10-MA 41-18272/PN-Q *MURDER INC* of the 449th BS/322nd BG

2
B-26B-25-MA 41-31814/ER-F *Bag of Bolts* of the 450th BS/322nd BG

3
B-26G-5-MA 43-34409/SS-M of the 451st BS/322nd BG

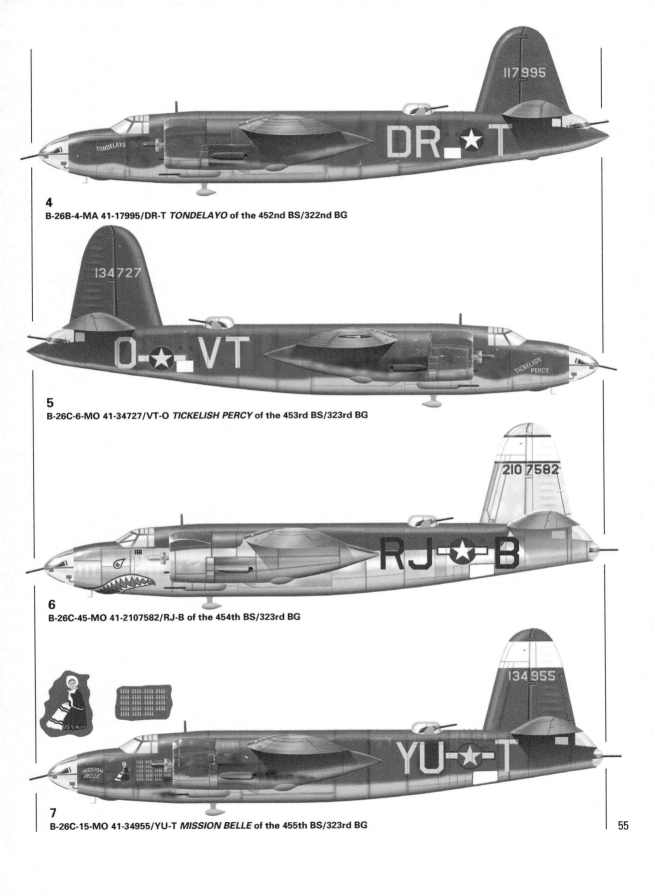

4
B-26B-4-MA 41-17995/DR-T *TONDELAYO* of the 452nd BS/322nd BG

5
B-26C-6-MO 41-34727/VT-O *TICKELISH PERCY* of the 453rd BS/323rd BG

6
B-26C-45-MO 41-2107582/RJ-B of the 454th BS/323rd BG

7
B-26C-15-MO 41-34955/YU-T *MISSION BELLE* of the 455th BS/323rd BG

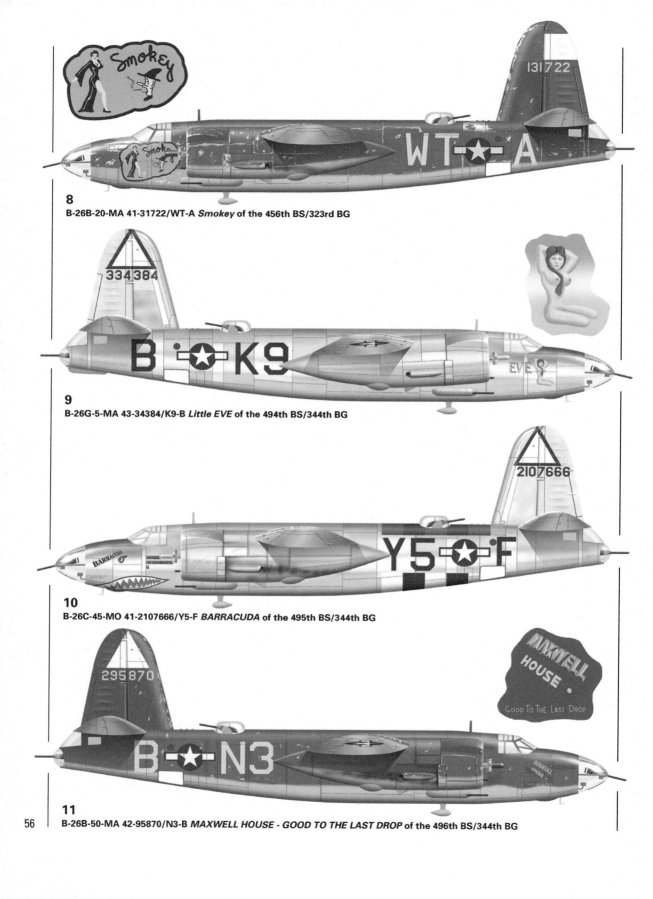

8
B-26B-20-MA 41-31722/WT-A *Smokey* of the 456th BS/323rd BG

9
B-26G-5-MA 43-34384/K9-B *Little EVE* of the 494th BS/344th BG

10
B-26C-45-MO 41-2107666/Y5-F *BARRACUDA* of the 495th BS/344th BG

11
B-26B-50-MA 42-95870/N3-B *MAXWELL HOUSE - GOOD TO THE LAST DROP* of the 496th BS/344th BG

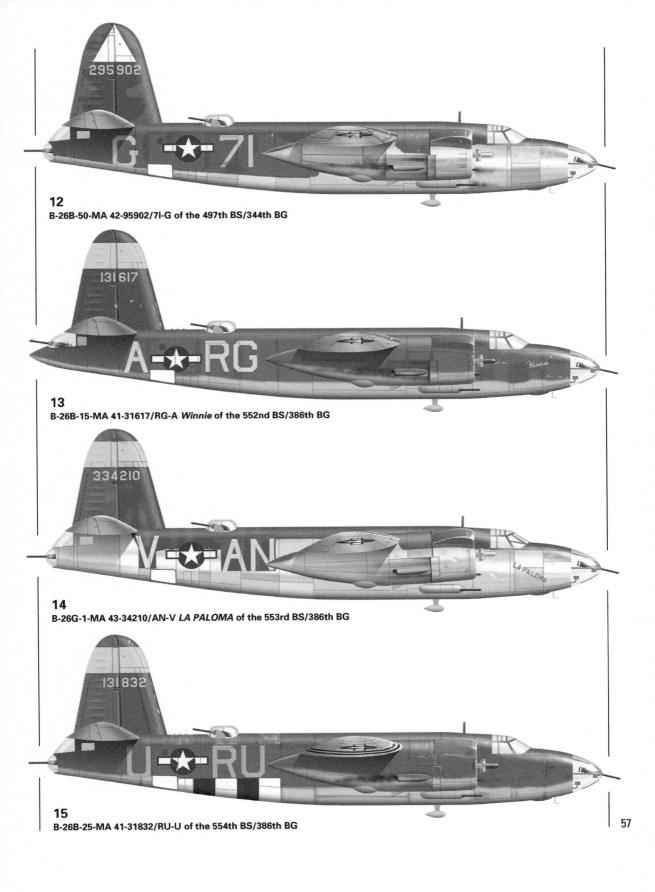

12
B-26B-50-MA 42-95902/7I-G of the 497th BS/344th BG

13
B-26B-15-MA 41-31617/RG-A *Winnie* of the 552nd BS/386th BG

14
B-26G-1-MA 43-34210/AN-V *LA PALOMA* of the 553rd BS/386th BG

15
B-26B-25-MA 41-31832/RU-U of the 554th BS/386th BG

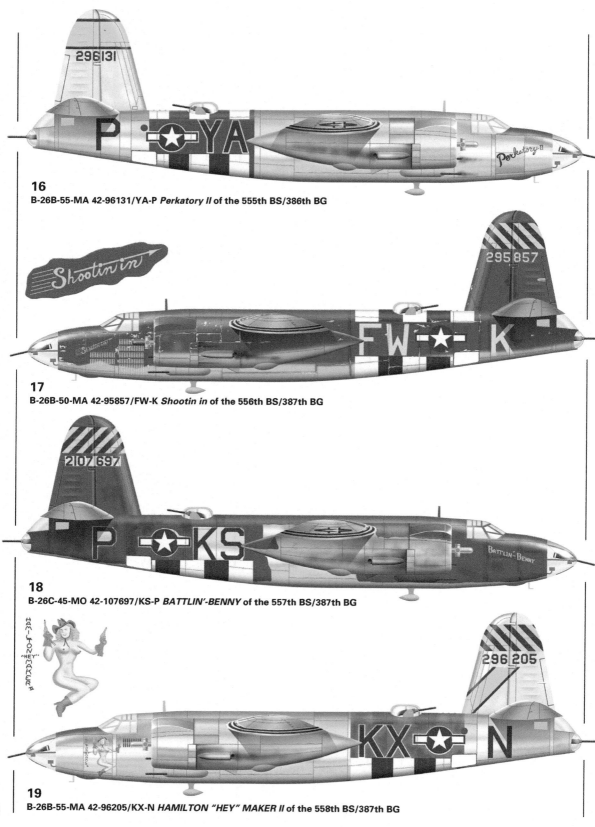

16
B-26B-55-MA 42-96131/YA-P *Perkatory II* of the 555th BS/386th BG

17
B-26B-50-MA 42-95857/FW-K *Shootin in* of the 556th BS/387th BG

18
B-26C-45-MO 42-107697/KS-P *BATTLIN'-BENNY* of the 557th BS/387th BG

19
B-26B-55-MA 42-96205/KX-N *HAMILTON "HEY" MAKER II* of the 558th BS/387th BG

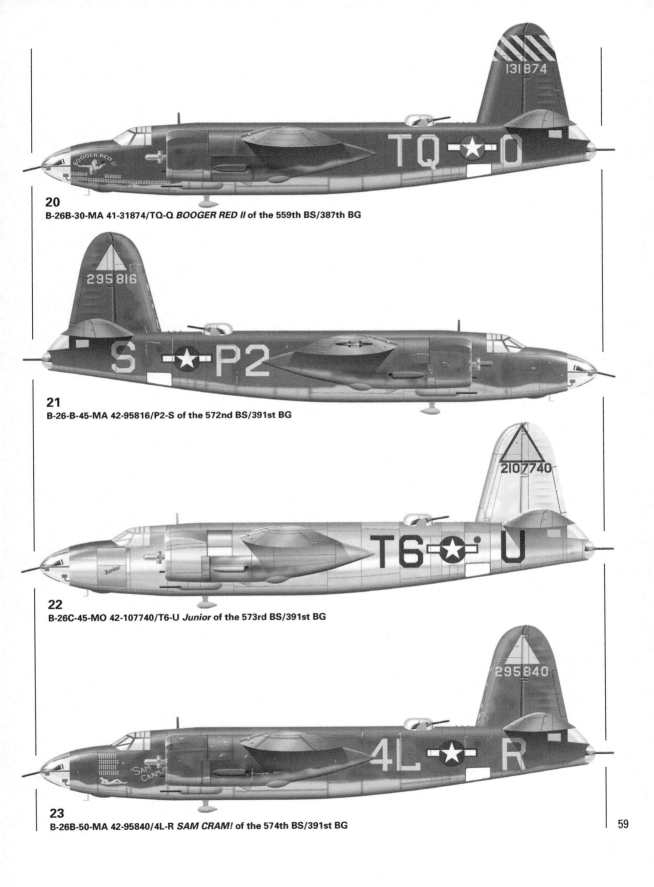

20
B-26B-30-MA 41-31874/TQ-Q *BOOGER RED II* of the 559th BS/387th BG

21
B-26-B-45-MA 42-95816/P2-S of the 572nd BS/391st BG

22
B-26C-45-MO 42-107740/T6-U *Junior* of the 573rd BS/391st BG

23
B-26B-50-MA 42-95840/4L-R *SAM CRAM!* of the 574th BS/391st BG

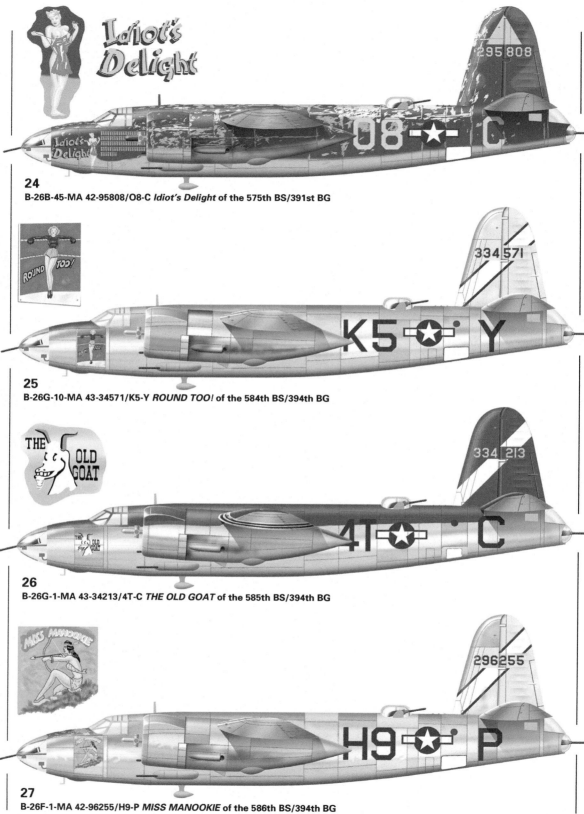

24
B-26B-45-MA 42-95808/O8-C *Idiot's Delight* of the 575th BS/391st BG

25
B-26G-10-MA 43-34571/K5-Y *ROUND TOO!* of the 584th BS/394th BG

26
B-26G-1-MA 43-34213/4T-C *THE OLD GOAT* of the 585th BS/394th BG

27
B-26F-1-MA 42-96255/H9-P *MISS MANOOKIE* of the 586th BS/394th BG

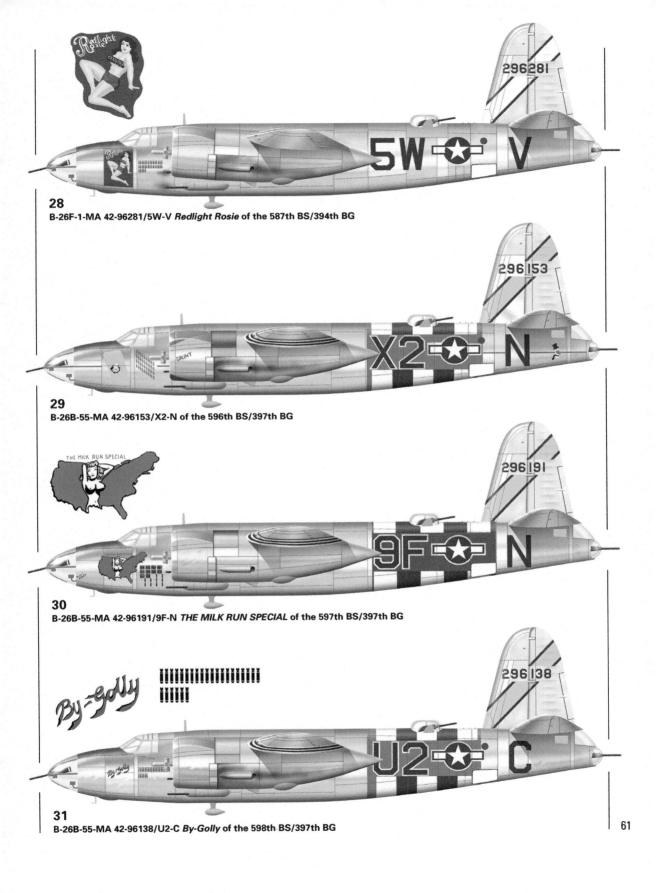

28
B-26F-1-MA 42-96281/5W-V *Redlight Rosie* of the 587th BS/394th BG

29
B-26B-55-MA 42-96153/X2-N of the 596th BS/397th BG

30
B-26B-55-MA 42-96191/9F-N *THE MILK RUN SPECIAL* of the 597th BS/397th BG

31
B-26B-55-MA 42-96138/U2-C *By-Golly* of the 598th BS/397th BG

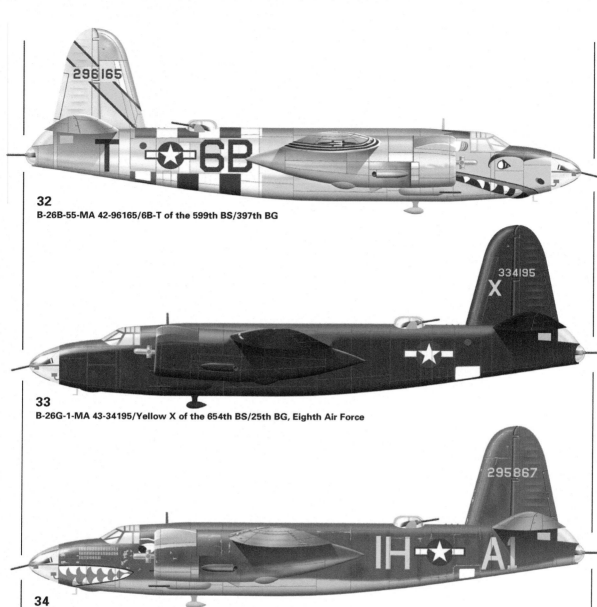

32
B-26B-55-MA 42-96165/6B-T of the 599th BS/397th BG

33
B-26G-1-MA 43-34195/Yellow X of the 654th BS/25th BG, Eighth Air Force

34
B-26B-50-MA 42-95867/IH-A1 of the 1st Pathfinder Squadron (Provisional)

1
Lt Ralph N Phillips, navigator with the 455th BS/323rd BG at Earls Colne, 1944

2
Capt Hugh Fletcher, bombardier with the 452nd BS/322nd BG, and his dog 'Salvo', at 'Andrews Field', 1944

3
SSgt 'Denny' McFarland, tail gunner with the 553rd BS/386th BG at Beaumont-sur-Oise, 1944

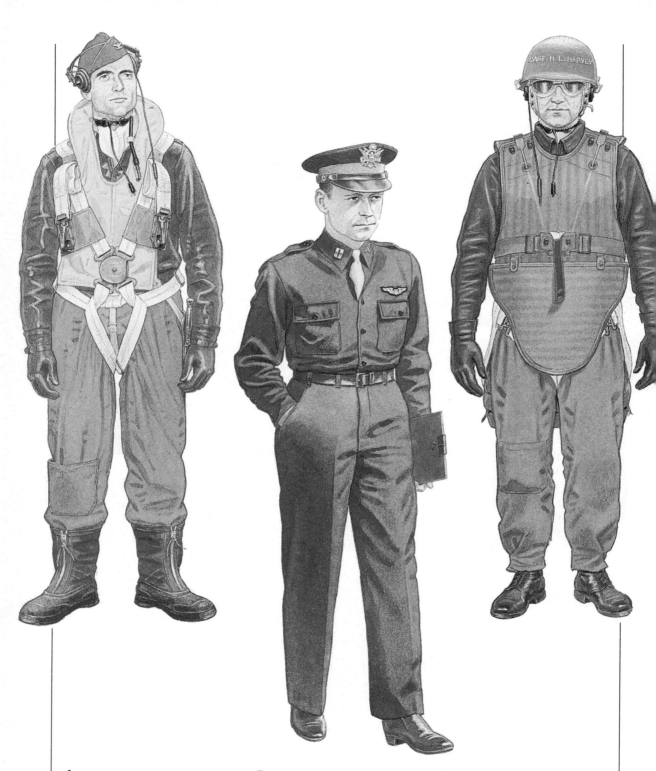

4
Col Jack Caldwell, CO of the 387th BG at Chipping Ongar in the early spring of 1944

5
Capt Louis Sebille, pilot with the 450th BS/322nd BG at 'Andrews Field', 1944

6
Capt Norman Harvey, pilot with the 449th BS/322nd BG at 'Andrews Field', 1944

BATTLE OF THE BULGE

Early December 1944 saw the weather reduce still further the number of days when the Marauder crews could count on clear conditions for accurate bombing. By the second week, with low temperatures bringing in ground fog, rain and more snow, some airfields had to all but shut down.

An oft-photographed aircraft was B-26F-1 42-96246 of the 559th BS/387th BG, coded TQ-H. This bomber has had its nose cone armament deleted (*Bruce Robertson*)

One advantage the groups flying Marauders had over other Allied medium bomber units was that their aircraft were fully 'winterised' as a result of the introduction of the larger engine air intakes on the B-26B-10. This effectively meant that little time was lost in engine ground-running prior to take-off when temperatures were low. However, the long-suffering groundcrews now had to contend with permanent open air dispersals for their charges, resulting in even the most routine of jobs falling foul to frozen fingers. Makeshift shelters were rigged to keep the most vulnerable areas of the Marauder from freezing, although on some days the bombers all but disappeared under a blanket of snow. Men then had to resort to the humble broom to sweep the stuff away, for any unnoticed build up of ice on flying surfaces could be highly dangerous. Canvas covers to protect Plexiglas sections and engines were part and parcel of a combat group's ground equipment inventory, and these, and many other items, accompanied the ground echelon unit during any move.

The Allied offensive all but stopped in the face of serious snow falls which carpeted most of the continent. At that time the Allied frontline extended from Nijmegen, in Holland, through Aachen, Liege Metz and Saarbrucken, down to the Swiss border. The Rhine had been reached, but not crossed. This last major obstacle would have to wait until conditions improved, for what the soldiers in the frontline were experiencing was one of the worst European winters for decades.

It was at that point on 16 December that Hitler launched his massive counter-offensive, succinctly codenamed *Wacht am Rhein* (*Watch on the Rhine*), through the fog-

A sight that was all too frequent at Marauder bases when German flak resulted in wrecked hydraulics, engine malfunction or other damage that necessitated a belly landing. Putting the ship down 'wheels up' was less risky if nosewheel damage was suspected, as a nose over could be nasty. Few photos have been published of aircraft of the 344th's 496th BS, which carried the code N3 – this one, N3-F came to grief in France (*Crow*)

Well on the way to becoming the all time record holder in terms of the number of sorties flown by a Western Allied combat aircraft (202 in total), *FLAK BAIT* of the 322nd BG tucks in close to younger sister-ship 43-34371 – a B-26G-5. An aircraft that lived up to its name by taking considerable battle damage, 41-31773 (the first B-26B-25) was not held in as high esteem as other veterans within the group (*USAF*)

Lt Jack K Havener created a minor sensation in a US cinema after the war when he saw 'his' Marauder being broken up in a newsreel report from Europe. He moaned loudly – much to the annoyance of other patrons – until the scenes of awful carnage ended! The ship in question was this B-26B-50 (42-95906/7I-H) of the 497th BS/344th BG, complete with a flak hole which Havener has his finger in. Shrapnel had entered here and subsequently hit him in the leg (*J Havener*)

shrouded Ardennes forest. Spearheaded by some 600 carefully hoarded tanks split between seven Panzer divisions, the advance parties of an infantry force numbering some 250,000 men moved forward to exploit the advantage provided by the weather, which effectively kept Allied aircraft from reacting for a vital 36 hours. Fog shrouded the first German movements of the day, aimed at thinly-held American positions. Striking swiftly out of the gloom, the panzers were able to make good progress, forcing a gap in the Allied frontline which soon bulged alarmingly at Malmedy, Bastogne and Dinant, on the river Meuse. Communications along the front were poor – a factor that aided the Germans – as the danger was not immediately realised.

Hitler gambled that a Panzer strike through the difficult Ardennes forest could duplicate a tactic similar to that deployed successfully against the French in 1940. To lead it he chose the same commander who had made such dramatic progress in France four years earlier – Field Marshal Karl von Runstedt. For well over a week, everything went well for the Germans. They were attacked from the air when there were breaks in the cloud long enough for targets to be identified, but in general the battle was going according to plan as the front broke open.

But then dawn on 23 December brought clearer conditions – a high pressure front coming in from the east enabled the weathermen to predict improved conditions for flying, although the situation would remain fluid and far from ideal. After last-minute meteorological checks, the Ninth Bomb Division finally gave the order for the 'mediums' to take-off, holding the fighters until there was more evidence that the weather really was breaking. When they did get off, the bomber crews knew that their sorties to cut the German supply lines were a matter of life or death to the beleaguered Allied troops. The 23rd consequently saw a huge interdiction effort against tactical targets, primarily those lying along five rail links. These lines were vital, for the Germans required vast quantities of fuel, spares, equipment and fresh troops to 'feed' the new frontline on the Western Front – and the railways had to cross bridges.

No less than 624 B-26s and A-20s were briefed to attack primary and secondary bridges at Mayen, Eller and Euskirchen, a viaduct at Ahrweiler, the railhead at Kyllburg and the marshalling yards at Prum. All the bridges were 50 miles from the front beyond the Eifel hills, and each one was assigned to two groups of Ninth Air Force B-26s. To ensure that the bombing was as accurate as possible, most 18-ship boxes were provided with a pathfinder – a much higher ratio than was normal.

Briefed to attack the Eller bridge, the 323rd sent out 30 aircraft (plus three B-26s tasked to drop 'Window') guided by three pathfinders. Take-off from Laon-Athies, in frosty conditions compounded by a damp haze, was slightly delayed due to one Marauder veering off the

runway and hitting a Cletrac tractor – there were no injuries in the crash but both aircraft and tractor were scrapped! The rest got away safely.

With good visibility in the target area, the group was bracketed by an enormous barrage of 88 mm shells, the German gunners taking equal advantage of clear sighting to range in on the bombers. Almost inevitably some chunks of flying steel made contact, and the machine flown by 1Lt Joseph C Bostick dropped out of formation in the target area. So much shrapnel struck Lt William H Eastwood's *Lady Luck III* that she had to stagger out of the target area and be abandoned over the 323rd's base. One flight leader, 1Lt Robert H Dowd, suddenly found his windscreen frosted over in the thin cold air, and he was forced to open the cockpit side window to see anything. Despite a 200-mph slipstream blasting into his face, Dowd successfully led his aircraft into the bomb run.

The accuracy of the flak was obvious even to the men on the ground when the group returned. Two B-26s were flying with an engine shut down, whilst one of the pathfinders landed but overshot and had badly damaged by the time it came to rest – at least 200 holes were counted. As well as the ultra-important bridges, Ninth BD's inner interdiction zone target list included various communications centres behind the Fifth Panzer Army – Waxweiler, Neuerburg and Luneberg among them. And reflecting the urgency of the situation following von Runstedt's surprise attack, some 417 'heavies' of the Eighth's 2nd Air Division were also temporarily placed under Ninth Air Force control to bomb targets in an outer

Down on an emergency strip (note the GIs) in France in late 1944 following battle damage, the nose of *BARRACUDA* is well enough known through published photographs, including a montage of 344th B-26 nose art made up during the war. Identified as B-26C-45 42-107666/Y5-F, the bomber had flown about 75 missions by the time this mishap occurred (*Crow*)

Included in almost every reference on the B-26, and quoted as being named the *Big Hairy Bird*, this striking Marauder had nose art that was comprised primarily of a yellow face, rather than white, as had long been thought. Originally assigned to the 599th BS/397th BG as 6B-T, it was transferred to the 387th BG's 558th BS shortly before the end of the war. There, it adopted the unit's tail markings, and presumably had the revised codes KX-T. The author still does not know if, or where, its distinctive name was applied! (*Hamlin via MacKay*)

Almost bereft of camouflage, apart from the regulation anti-glare panels on the nose and inner facing engine cowlings, B-26F-1 42-96288/X2-Q of the 397th was flown by a pilot named Hoch, who was presumably holding the ship steady while his bombardier sighted for the release of its load of 1000-lb bombs (*Crow*)

Standing by to 'walk through' the propellers in order to clear the plugs prior to engine start, the ground-crew assigned to look after B-26C-45 (42-107673) of the 572nd BS/391st BG may later have been able to enjoy a little time in the sun judging by the shadows. Once a mission was underway, these men could relax until the aircraft returned, although there was always work to do at a busy operational airfield (*Hamlin via MacKay*)

interdiction zone lying west of the Rhine. No effort was spared to stop German supplies reaching the battlefield.

With the sudden re-opening of the Allied air campaign, there were so many bombers in the air that the fighter resources were stretched. This effectively meant that some 'mediums' would have to brave the defences alone. Up to this point in the invasion, B-26 crews had not been threatened by the *Jagdwaffe* due to Allied air superiority. Indeed, some crews had never seen an enemy fighter in the air. Two days before Christmas many of them saw enough to last an entire combat tour.

MASSACRE

The German attack plan for *Wacht am Rhein* had included a substantial Luftwaffe support force, whose order of battle numbered 1492 fighters. Amongst the units based within range of the Ninth Division's medium bombers on 23 December were III. and IV.(*Sturm*)/JG 3 at Gutersloh, Lippspringe and Paderborn; JG 1, which was dispersed at Twente, Drop and Rhein in Holland; and JG 11, then using Biblis, Zellhausen and Grossostheim. *Jagdgeschwader* 1 and 11, equipped with Bf 109G/Ks, usually flew together as a combined unit, whilst the component *Staffeln* of IV./JG 3 represented the original *Sturmgruppe* equipped with well-armoured Fw 190A-8s, which were usually sent against US heavy bombers (see Osprey's *Aircraft of the Aces 9 Focke-Wulf Aces of the Western Front* by John Weal for further details). The pilots were about to demonstrate how effective the 30 mm Mk 108 cannon fitted to their aircraft could also be against 'mediums'.

For the Marauder crews, a maximum effort on the scale of 23 December had not been seen since the D-Day invasion. Action began early, with the 391st BG sending 31 bombers (led by a pathfinder) to attack the Ahrweiler viaduct. Flak was intense, and the pathfinder ship was crippled before the target was reached. Once over the viaduct, most crews found it all but obscured by cloud, with the flak putting up a terrific barrage.

Leading the second box, Capt Edward M Jennsen flew to the briefed fighter rendezvous point, only to find the Marauders were still alone. He nevertheless plunged into the flak protecting the viaduct, chagrined to see that the bombers' approach was way off. Jennsen then turned what remained of his force (five B-26s already having gone down) onto the correct approach and led them in again. With his own aircraft on fire, the captain had the satisfaction of knowing that the bombs had at least been aimed squarely at the viaduct. The crews knew how important the mission was, but the missed approach took precious time to correct – time enough for the B-26s to be plotted by enemy radar.

No friendly fighters were in the vicinity when the *Jagdwaffe* hit the 391st shortly after 1135 with about 60 Fw 190s, allowing the German pilots to choose their targets with care. Designed to withstand all but the most concentrated bursts of machine-gun fire at point-blank range, the Fw 190A-8 was a formidable opponent. On average, pilots had found that it took just three hits in a vital area to down a heavy bomber with the Mk 108 cannon. Just how much firepower it took to destroy a Marauder was probably not known at the time. They were about to find out.

The German pilots managed to break through the tight American formations and achieve enough dispersal to give themselves room to manoeuvre. They proceeded to destroy the bombers piecemeal, taking just nine minutes to shoot down sixteen Marauders.

Bomber pilots took violent evasive action and the gunners fought like tigers, their claims reaching as high as the number of Marauders lost, plus three damaged and a further 16 probably destroyed. But in reality the battle was one-sided. The 322nd, which did have an escort in the shape of 392nd FS Lightnings, clashed with the *Jagdwaffe* near its target at Euskirchen bridge. In eight desperate minutes, Bf 109s, Marauders and P-38s fought it out. Three B-26s, including a pathfinder, went down and a fourth, turned into a flying wreck by enemy fire, was later abandoned near Sedan. One P-38 was shot down in return for claims of four Bf 109s.

Bloody, but unbowed, the 391st was able to successfully execute an afternoon mission by sending off 21 aircraft – fortunately the German fighters were occupied elsewhere tackling the ever-increasing number of Allied aircraft appearing over the battlefield. Soon German losses began to escalate to the sort of level had been reached before the Battle of the Bulge began. These could be ill-afforded, for although aircraft could be readily replaced, pilots could not.

That the *Jadgwaffe* was active only in certain areas was shown by the experience of the 344th (attacking Mayen) and 386th (attacking Nideggen), for neither group was intercepted. However, at the end of their blackest day in terms of aerial loss, some 35 Marauders from the 322nd, 387th, 391st and 397th BGs, plus a solitary A-20, had been shot down, with a further 182 B-26s sustaining various categories of damage.

Pilots of IV./JG 3 actually claimed 27 Marauder victories in the space of nine minutes' combat between 1138 and 1147. In addition, three Thunderbolts were also downed, which took them a further five minutes. All their victims are believed to have been from the luckless 391st BG, which sustained the largest number of losses in aerial combat. A degree of over-claiming

Early on in the AAF's bomber offensive over Europe it was said to be unlucky to change an aircraft's name, but that 'rule' didn't seem to apply in Marauder groups. Numerous B-26s were re-named, or given different artwork, with a case in point being B-26B-55 42-96153/X2-N of the 596th BS/397th BG. Traces of its former name can just be seen above its new artwork, which reflected its revised nickname of *The Joker*. The angled presentation of the bomb log was non-standard (*Crow*)

This unusual presentation of crew nicknames and surnames was seen on B-26G-5 (almost certainly 43-34330) *I'll Get By*, which belonged to the 394th when it was based at Cambrai. 'Singleton' and 'Leask' were most likely the pilot and co-pilot, respectively (*Crow*)

Lt Robert B Gaver's *CENTENARIAN* was a B-26B-55 of the 394th BG which had put 113 missions on the board by early 1945 (*Crow*)

Old soldiers do die sometimes. On 27 November 1944, combat veteran B-26B-16 41-31650 *Miss Mary* of the 553rd BS was totally written off in a heavy crash landing which broke the fuselage aft of the wing. This aircraft seems to have never had the yellow 386th BG tail band applied (*T Bivens*)

occurred, but each individual '*abschluss*' was filed, and presumably accepted, by JG 3's intelligence officers. The most successful pilots were each credited with two B-26s, these being; Lt Siegfried Muller of 16.*Staffel* (12th and 13th victories); Uffz Kurt Bolz (third and fourth victories) of 13.*Staffel*; and Uffz Werner Martin of IV.*Gruppenstab* (first and second kills).

The appearance of so many German interceptors surprised the American fighter pilots, who suddenly had their hands full. In some cases they were drawn away from the bombers and given little choice but to combat their adversaries. Equally, there were enough Fw 190s and Bf 109s available for dual attacks to be made on the fighters and 'mediums' operating in different sectors. Among the other German units in action that day was the Bf 109-equipped I./JG 77 – at 1108 Lt Kuhdorf of 1.*Staffel* claimed a single B-26 'over the Ardennes region' for his 16th kill of the war.

The furious pace, and scale, of the 23 December air battle was the most intense that Marauder crews were ever to face against the German fighter force in the ETO. The day was also the worst in terms of B-26 losses for the entire war. Even if such German successes had become increasingly rare over the preceding months, this action graphically proved that there was little room for complacency, and the possibility of the *Jagdwaffe* disrupting future medium bomber operations remained a factor throughout the Ardennes counter-offensive. Dire projections were made by Allied commnaders that if this rate of medium bomber loss continued, Ninth BD would be wiped out – on 24 December steps were taken to prevent that occurring when a massive blitz on German airfields was launched.

Among the positive results of the missions flown on 23 December was the strike by the 397th BG on the bridge at Eller. Some 33 B-26s took off from Peronne, with all crews fully aware that their target was an important one. The bridge was the only point at which the rail link from the Ruhr to Dinant, in Belgium, crossed the Moselle River, and the Germans were frantically despatching westbound trains loaded with vital supplies for the Wehrmacht along this route.

Flak clawed at the lead box of bombers on their target approach. Although there was no escort, pathfinders dropped 'Window' to obliterate gun-laying radar as they led the 397th through the cloud. Two B-26s were quickly shot down, but just before the initial point, the clouds parted long enough for the bombardiers to sight the bridge. Another Marauder fell away. The

The port side of *Miss Mary* reveals that she had flown at least 100 missions in her short career – which was true of so many Ninth Air Force Marauders. The circumstances of the crash are unknown, but it is assumed that the aircraft was on a non-combat flight on the day it was wrecked. All guns have been removed, either before the flight or after the crash as a normal safety precaution (*T Bivens*)

An example of the deadly winter weather of 1944-45 that sparked Hitler's last land offensive on the Western Front, now known as the notorious Battle of the Bulge. When the weather let them, the Ninth's 'mediums' pounded targets behind the front to cut off the enemy's life blood in the form of men, materials and fuel. An idea of the conditions on all bases within range of the Ardennes can be gauged from this shot of 386th BG aircraft seen at their Clastres home around Christmas 1944 (*USAF*)

seconds of the bomb run seemed like weeks. Then the bombs fell, bang on target. The vital bridge was cut.

Enemy fighters intercepted the second box of 397th aircraft while it was on the bomb run – now it was up to the gunners. Bombardiers hunched over their sights, flying the aircraft just as though they had the control yoke in their hands. Fighter attacks intensified, and individual bombers trailed streamers of white gun smoke as they fought back.

German cannon and machine-gun fire began taking its deadly toll as seven Marauders succumbed to repeat passes by an estimated 40-50 Fw 190s and Bf 109s, although tight formation keeping prevented the losses from being far worse – gunners claimed 4-4-8. It seems most likely that the 397th was hit by a combined JG 1/JG 11 force, component *Staffeln* of which flew both the Fw 190A-8 and the Bf 109G-14. What might be questioned is the victory claims made by the pilots – no less than 24 B-26s were credited. Modest though their own claims were, American bomber gunners were clearly responsible for some of the German losses. In total, the two *Jagdgeschwader* lost 11 pilots killed and 45 aircraft written off to all causes on 23 December.

Weather brought its own lethal challenges in addition to those associated with combat. This 397th BG B-26 was written off at Cambrai on 13 January 1945, but the degree of damage suffered before it crashed is unknown (*Crow*)

Back at base, the 397th's groundcrews counted the holes. Only eight B-26s could be given a clean bill of health, with the rest requiring urgent repairs before they flew again. The group had 71 men killed or wounded in the day's action, and for its determination to complete its mission against heavy odds, the 397th was awarded a DUC. Also honoured with a Unit Citation was the 387th, which had attacked targets at Mayen and Prum. Fighter attacks had also marginally reduced the latter group's bombing effort, between 15 and 29 Bf 109s attacked and shot down four Marauders, including a pathfinder ship – these were the first losses suffered by the group in some 520 sorties.

Pathfinders had had a rough time of it ever since the Ninth had intro-

More often than not B-26s came home with evidence of enemy intent, giving crews food for thought. One that might have crossed this crew's collective minds was the wisdom of removing the front guns! In fact if it was flak that had inflicted this splinter damage, then a 'couple of 'fifties up front' wouldn't have been of much use – a fighter attack, however, would have been another matter entirely. Few details pertaining to this crew, or their unit, are known, but the release date of the photo was 1 January 1945 (*USAF*)

duced bomb-on-leader methods, for the enemy was well aware of their importance at the head of the combat boxes. When the 322nd visited the Euskirchen bridge, 50 Bf 109s appeared on the scene and promptly shot down the lead pathfinder aircraft. Turning their attention to the second pathfinder, they succeeded in damaging it so badly that it was all but useless. A third B-26 (a regular 322nd BG ship) fell away before Allied fighters showed up to beat the enemy interceptors back. A fourth bomber was lost when flak sited around the bridge opened up with a vengeance, whilst a fifth had to be abandoned while returning home due to battle damage.

Despite an improvement in the weather towards the end of the month, atmospheric conditions still varied enough to adversely affect operations by some medium bomber groups. However, it gradually became clear that von Runstedt's highly optimistic Ardennes offensive was losing momentum. Tactical bombers were able to continue pounding targets in the inner interdiction zone, strikes by 350+ 'mediums' – about half the total B-26 force available to the Ninth – being a regular occurrence. When weather permitted, the command was able to despatch more than double this number, such as on 26-27 December when 879 aircraft (mostly Marauders) blasted the German rail network. For its contribution to this major effort, the 323rd won a DUC covering the four-day period between the 24th and 27th. Luftwaffe attacks also noticeably dwindled under the renewed onslaught from Allied fighters.

By that time the command had been able to prove that the Douglas A-26 Invader would be a worthy successor to both the B-26 and A-20 through its combination of the not dissimilar roles of medium bombing and low-level attack. After an initial period of combat evaluation by the 386th BG in September, Invaders had belatedly joined this group and the 323rd, 344th and 391st BGs, all of which gradually relinquished their Marauders as crew conversion proceeded within a framework of continuing combat operations.

The high number of B-26s damaged during missions in support of the Ardennes counter-offensive combined with the increasing delivery of new Invaders to see numerous Marauders transferred between groups to maintain the required strength for tactical commitments. In most cases these aircraft were welcome replacements – the pace of operations also led to some interesting dual paint schemes, with the new owners applying

Still serving despite no longer being part of the frontline, short-tail B-26B-4 41-18022 *El Diablo* was passed from the 322nd BG (where it had flown as ER-U with the 450th BS) to the 3rd Combat Crew Replacement Center (CCRC). It was photographed on a flight from Base Air Depot 2 at Warton on 29 January 1945, 1Lt Jack Knight being at the controls. At least four of its guns have been retained, and the code WS is believed to have been allocated to the 3rd CCRC. The individual aircraft letter is I (*H Holmes*)

With 21 sorties to her credit, *El Diablo* did not fly on the first Imjuiden mission with the 322nd – which leaves a question about the three horizontal red bomb symbols indicating 'zero feet' sorties stencilled forward of the name. These may have been chalked up when the group was flying early missions with Eighth Air Support Command (*H Holmes*)

their markings over those that identified former operators. Full repainting normally had to wait for a lull in operations, or a major overhaul, but on some aircraft it appeared that the job was never completed! Dual markings (including those of the Twelfth AAF aircraft passed onto Ninth groups) still remained visible when the Marauders were scrapped.

At first the Invader was treated with the natural scepticism inevitable with any new type. Primarily replacing the A-20 rather than the B-26, the Marauder groups saw no need for a substitute for the aircraft that had thoroughly proved itself, and had bred a fierce loyalty amongst its flyers. The men who 'crewed the ship' were at the core of the bomber's solid reputation, to which all the combat groups had contributed. Marauder units had turned in consistently accurate bombing records against difficult, well defended, targets. Indeed, had the 'mediums' been unable to remove these from the path of Allied troops, the ground war would have undoubtedly been far more arduous and lengthy.

To offset any loss of bombing accuracy due to the introduction of the relatively unfamiliar A-26, it was sound policy to retain a number of Marauders, and their experienced bombardiers, to lead flights of Invaders during the transition period. But the inevitability of having to master a replacement type was shouldered by innumerable flyers during the war, and some of the Ninth's B-26 crews were no exception. Actually, once they had checked out in it, even some 'dyed-in-the-wool' Marauder champions had to agree that Douglas had not done a bad job with their sleek attack bomber. It flew further than a B-26, and had an impressive single-engined performance – a quality that impressed the men who would have to fly it.

Irrespective of the aircraft they were flying, there was no question of the Ninth's tactical bomber units giving the Germans any respite. Crews managed conversion to the A-26 with minimum time out of the line, just as base changes were rarely

Winter's mantle soon lost all its charm if you had to live in a tent and service aeroplanes in sub-zero temperatures at four in the morning, knowing that the better accommodation on the airfield had probably been bombed by your own aircraft! That was a common experience of the Marauder groups based on the continent during the last winter of the war, as exemplified by B-26G-5 43-34413 of the 386th at Beaumont-sur-Oise, with a decidedly draughty hanger behind it (*USAF*)

On 22 January 1945 the 387th carried out a blind bombing attack on a railway bridge near Simmern, south of Koblenz, and a Ninth Air Force photographer was came along for the mission to capture on film the moment that a box of B-26s of the 556th BS released their loads. Subsequent reconnaissance coverage confirmed that the bombs had cut the north-west approach to the bridge, damaging an abutment and collapsing one span. An embankment and tracks further down the line were also hit (*USAF*)

allowed to interrupt missions a second longer than was necessary. And while the ground situation remained critical, Allied airpower took advantage of the slightest break in the weather.

The stubborn American resistance at Bastogne helped to break the back of the German attack – over-stretched, and running low on fuel and other war-sustaining supplies, the panzers were gradually whittled down through a combination of armoured and aerial attacks until they no longer posed a threat. Allied materiel and personnel resources were almost infinite compared with the German logistical situation, and once airpower had been able to stem the flow of supplies, von Runstedt's gamble was doomed.

Help from above – in more than one sense – soon enabled the Allied ground forces to gear up for a final push into Germany, secure in the knowledge that their progress would be as smooth as possible. With its ambitious last ditch offensive stalled, and vehicles of all kinds backed up for miles in front of shattered bridges, the remnants of the Wehrmacht were decimated.

Fighter-bombers had long been adept at blocking convoy movement by destroying the leading and trailing tanks, or soft-skinned vehicles, whereupon those trapped in the centre of the column could be strafed by fighters and bombed by 'mediums' in almost leisurely fashion at major choke points. Fearful carnage marked the end of the Battle of the Bulge, the *coup de grace* occurring on 22 January when the 387th and 394th BGs send their B-26s against road bridges. Crews led in by four pathfinders found traffic jams of up to 1500 vehicles.

January as a whole represented the culmination of months of hard fighting. Although 20 'mediums' were lost due to enemy action and weather, operations were possible on 19 days, during which the Ninth BD launched 3938 sorties, 2540 of which were judged to be effective.

On 15 January the Ninth Air Force marked a major milestone – B-26s had, by that date, dropped 100,000 tons of bombs on enemy targets. It had taken some 80,000 sorties, and seen the loss of about 300 aircraft.

Many of February's sorties were flown in support of Operation *Clarion*, the planned paralysis of the German transport network behind the frontline for a period of 24 hours. Western Germany was split into sectors, with each being assigned to an air force – either the Ninth, Eighth, the RAF or a special unit known as the 42nd Wing. Gen Anderson's bombers were given 80 possible targets, from which 50 would be attacked. A new innovation adopted specially for this mission was the use of Marauders as ground strafers, permission being given to crews to drop down to deck level with their fighter cover to strafe enemy targets of opportunity once they had released their load – the *Jagdwaffe* was now an all but spent force.

Permission to take their B-26s down to strafe on 22 February brought a mixed reaction. Some pilots thought this would bring certain death, whilst others saw more positive aspects to the new role – flying a 'P-26' would certainly be a satisfying way to round out a mission after sitting at medium altitude and taking it from the flak. When the combat reports came in, it was found that the participants couldn't wait to do it again. It appears that strafing was allowed, circumstances permitting, until the German collapse. There was some irony associated with this new role, for Martin had anticipated the need for just such an aircraft. Indeed, the company had even gone so far as to convert an early-production B-26 into a 'dedicated' strafer, but it was never ordered.

Aside from the strafing role, *Clarion* was essentially 'business a usual' for the medium bomber crews who, in four-and-a-half hours, struck 46 of the 50 targets, plus four secondary ones. In small units sometimes consisting of only three to six aircraft, the Ninth's element of the *Clarion* force made bridges its primary objective. It lost just one aircraft.

Improving weather, and the accelerated pace of the ground war now rushing towards a climax, demanded a dedicated effort from the tactical air forces. Ranging further east, the Ninth offered material help to the advancing Red Army by bombing a series of bridges on rail lines linking Cologne and Frankfurt. This helped delay the Wehrmacht reinforcements so desperately needed to stem the tide of tanks, guns and men pouring into Germany from the east.

During February the 'mediums' flew 6624 sorties for the loss of 67 aircraft, most of the latter falling to flak – as attested to by the fact that an additional 1362 bombers were damaged. German flak artillery, including vast numbers of the notoriously reliable '88', was concentrated around the remaining targets within a shrinking perimeter. Some crews consequently found this to be the most demanding period of the war when it came to bombing accurately through veritable walls of anti-aircraft fire.

On 9 February, the 323rd BG had moved to Denain, this French base

PUGNACIOUS of the 587th BS/ 394th BG is about to become considerably heavier at Cambrai in early 1945. Although the aircraft's manual said that the Marauder was 'red lined' at 37,000 lb all up weight, combat units regularly took off at 40,000 lb without difficulty – but they monitored engine performance very closely indeed as the ship gathered flying speed (*Crow*)

This photograph was probably taken at around the same time as the previous shot, group-mate *OLD GOAT* (alias B-26G-1 43-34213) making a nice profile while it waits for the HE bombs and incendiaries stacked beside it to be loaded. Standing next to the *'GOAT* in the 585th BS dispersal area at Cambrai at that time was a B-26G-5 43-34413, which had been transferred in from the 323rd following the latter's conversion to A-26s (*Crow*)

Boasting another of those disparaging, but no less affectionate, nicknames, the *'GOAT* is bedecked in a cockpit cover to keep out the worst of the weather. Luckily Martin designer Peyton Magruder's ingenuity in perfecting curved windshield panels made the pilot's visibility marginally better in freezing conditions than conventional flat panels (*Crow*)

being the group's last home before hostilities ceased. This relocation was just one in a series of movements by Ninth Air Force medium bomber groups that was to last until early May. By then, these units were flying B-26G-20s, which proved to be the last example of the Marauder to see wartime service. The production line ran to 893 examples, ending with the G-21 and G-25, although few of these reached Europe. The longevity of the Marauder resulted in many veterans of earlier production blocks flying alongside the youngsters, these early machines being distinguishable by their stepped rear gun position and, likely as not, a camouflage finish that was less than pristine – in stark contrast to the bare metal finish of the latest 'twisted wing' B-26s to arrive in the ETO.

By 16 February the base teletypes were spewing out lists of targets contained in a location that had long been notorious among Allied heavy bomber crews – the Ruhr valley. What was now proposed was a series of tactical thrusts aimed at further disrupting Germany's industrial base so as to alleviate the pressure opposing a spring campaign designed to end with the Western Allies linking up with the Red Army. If successful, the 'Battle of the Ruhr' would isolate the Rhine battle sector. For the 'mediums', the main effort would be against 11 key bridges east of the river, plus rail lines and road networks in between.

Between 16 February and the second week of March, Ninth BD bombers set their sights on scores of bridges, junctions, stations, rail yards, ordnance depots and motor repair facilities. The result was a gigantic swath of destruction reaching halfway to Berlin, and taking in Koblenz, Wiesbaden, Cologne and Hannover. Dozens of towns, villages and even hamlets had their local transport system completely wrecked.

Medium bomber raids under the *Clarion* plan did not go unchallenged by the *Jagdwaffe*, however, for on 22 February, Oberfeldwebel Paul Wittke of 13./JG 27 claimed a B-26 south-west of Munster for his 21st victory. Two days later Feldwebel Erich Heinrich of the same *Staffel* shot down a B-26 in the vicinity of Dusseldorf for his first aerial victory. Attacks on small formations of unescorted 'mediums', if not single bombers, enabled such quick kills to be scored before Allied escorts could react. Many such victories were accumulated when individuals on both sides adopted the time-honoured creed of the fighter pilot.

77

DEADLY ADVERSARIES

Reports of sightings of German rocket- and jet-powered fighters were widely circulated among Ninth Air Force combat groups, but until 6 February 1945, none had been observed by medium bomber crews. On that day eye-witnesses aboard aircraft of the 323rd BG reported a single Me 262 that fortunately did not attack. The jet merely flew under the B-26 formation, which was in the process of attacking targets at Berg/Gladbach. Nobody knew the extent to which the Germans had been able to disperse jet fighter production, or how effective they would be in combat, but the threat they posed was taken very seriously.

More familiar Luftwaffe fighters made some of their last attacks of the war on B-26s on 21 February 1945 when the 394th BG was intercepted by around 20 Fw 190s of II./JG 26 on a *Freie Jagd*. Ground control alerted the fighters while they were airborne, and the German pilots were surprised to find the bombers without an escort.

The group, who were operating that day against the rail bridge at Vlotho, had already experienced some difficulties up to this point in the sortie, with one box having lost an aircraft to flak over the target and the rest straying off course. They were east of Arnhem when the Fw 190s hit them, Unteroffizier Walter Stumpf of 7.*Staffel* shooting down a bomber and watching its crew bail out. Two other B-26s succumbed to the attack, whilst a futher four made it home despite being badly damaged by enemy fire. One crew from the 587th and three from the 585th had been lost.

Attacking ahead of the US Seventh Army on 15 March, Ninth BD sent 400 Marauders, Invaders and Havocs against four communications centres, including Neunkirchen. Main roads, intersections and buildings were subject to 365 tons of high explosive and incendiaries, some of them dropped by *Redlight Rosie* of the 394th BG (*USAF*)

Allied tanks waiting on the banks of the Rhine were finally able to cross the last great natural barrier to the heart of the Third Reich on 7 March. As the Shermans rumbled across the the railway bridge at Remagen (the only intact crossing point), the pincer movement became unstoppable. Germany was being crushed between 'jaws' formed by the Western Allies in the south and the Red Army in the East.

Remagen became a magnet for the Luftwaffe, who made desperate bomber attacks in an attempt to destroy this one remaining bridge. On 11 March Gen Anderson sent his 'mediums' out to destroy the four Luftwaffe airfields within range of the river.

In the air, that part of the Luftwaffe fighter force flying conventional fighters finally appeared to have been neutralised by its crippling losses firstly over the Ardennes, and then in the New Year's Day attack on Allied airfields. Hitler now had little choice but to play his final card in the form of the jet interceptor. Only the Me 262 was a practical proposition in this respect, and although production had been given an eleventh hour priority in 1944, scant success had been achieved. Medium bombers were never a priority target for the German jets, but with the increase of Me 262 sorties more frequent sightings were reported. Allied fighter escort to B-17 and B-24 raids was then so strong that the tactic of using jets to attack only heavy bomber formations had to be all but abandoned – the Me 262s rarely had the chance to get into firing position before they were chased off by dozens of P-47s and P-51s. To merely survive, the German pilots were often obliged to attack anything that came into their sights.

Nevertheless, the most advanced fighter in the world was demonstrably capable of causing a swift and terrible execution to a piston-engined bomber. On the ground, Gen Eisenhower took the controversial decision to cut Germany in two, thus leading the Anglo-American armies towards the Ruhr and Leipzig, and abandoning Berlin to the Red Army. In the event progress was good, with German resistance becoming noticeably weaker and less organised.

Thousands of Wehrmacht soldiers, including old men and boys, surrendered rather than die where they stood. Prisoners attested to the 'living hell' of the constant pounding by Allied aircraft. In the meantime, the Ninth's tactical fighters had moved onto German soil in substantial strength, with some of the medium bomber groups moving up to again shorten the range to their targets. Late in March the 322nd took up residence at Le Culot, in Belgium, this being its second continental base since moving to Beauvais the previous September.

Operations continued much as before: medium altitude attacks on communications targets was the daily fare of the crews. Some B-26 groups condoned the removal of some guns to save weight and increase speed – in many Marauders

It can be assumed that 'Rosie's portrait graced the armour plate panel of B-26F-1 42-96281 for all 108 combat missions it flew between 13 June 1944 and VE-Day. This late 1944 view shows it still with some missions to come, its pilot at the time being Lt J V Roy. 'Rosie posed on a grey painted panel, which contrasted well with her black hair and red panties. Pasting of 'modesty strips' over nude female nose-art was quite common (Crow)

Flak remained troublesome for Allied bombers right to the end. Haltern was the target when this 394th BG B-26G-15, nicknamed *Draggin Lady*, was nearly bracketed by the 'stuff' on 22 March 1945. This mission coincided with the group's first anniversary in combat, and it was a rough one, for two aircraft were lost. Quite often the worst result of flak was shrapnel splinters, which could, and frequently did, cause numerous incapacitating, and painful, wounds to bomber crews (Crow)

Groundcrews patched about 1000 holes in *Flak Bait* before she was finally stood down at the end of the war, having survived some 202 missions, including six decoy sorties. With a record like this, the crew felt it highly appropriate to put a BIG bomb on the log when the double century was reached – nobody ever actually amended it to read 202. Fred Macauza is at the extreme left, with bombardier O J 'Red' Redmond second from left, wearing a cap. The remaining individuals in this group are medical personnel on detachment with the 322nd (*Crow*)

the nose area had long since been de-armed primarily as a practical move to give the bombardier more room to work. When the bulky Norden sight was installed below the breech and ammunition tanks of the centre-line .50 cal gun, the nose cone, which was never exactly roomy, became quite cramped, especially for a big man in flying clothing.

Lightening the Marauder in this way also gave the bomber a better turn of speed both into and out of the target area, thus giving flak gunners less chance of obtaining a 'bead'. The possibility that Luftwaffe fighters could fall on lesser-armed bomber formations was an accepted risk – not that a B-26 devoid of all of its nose guns was exactly defenceless, for it still had ten 'fifties if trouble appeared. If the worst happened, and a Marauder dropped out of formation before releasing its bombs, it lost altitude at the alarming rate of 2000 ft per minute – jettisoning its bombs (and everything else moveable if there was time) arrested the rate to half this figure.

Florrenes, in Belgium, became the new base for the 344th BG, which became operational from there on 2 April. A week later the Invaders of the 386th occupied St Trond, and the 391st, also now converted from B-26s

Flak Bait leads a trio of 322nd B-26s to Magdeburg to complete her 200th mission on 17 April 1945, by which time the aircraft had flown 177,460 miles and consumed some 157,850 gallons of gasoline! The bare metal ship is 42-107664 PN-A, nicknamed *Je Reviens* ('I Return'), which flew 69 missions and had *Fin la Guerre* applied to the prominent black panel at the end of the bomb log. Above *Flak Bait* is 43-34371 PN-X, which appears to have carried a number of names, with PN-D (believed to have been 41-31822) bringing up the rear (*USAF*)

A well posed portrait of B-26G-25 44-68161/H9-Q of the 586th BS/ 394th BG at Villacoublay – one of the Paris airfields – in April 1945. The aircraft has the rear fuselage tray fitted to collect empty shell cases from the rear gun position, a modification that seemed to be rarer on Ninth AF Marauders than those of the Twelfth (*H Holmes*)

The port side of H9-Q reveals both nose-art on the armour plate panel and the fact that the ex-344th or 391st tail triangle has been painted over on both sides. Taken at Nurnberg, Germany, later in the war, this view also shows that the aircraft had also been stripped of its guns since its move from France (*Crow*)

to A-26s under group commander Col Gerald E Williams, went to Asch on the 20th of the month. The latter had taken charge of the group before it left for the ETO, and he was to remain in command until its last mission on 3 May 1945.

Ninth BD had been able to send out 200 to 350 medium and light bombers on most recent missions, and on 3 April some 220 had sortied, along with 12 'Window' aircraft, to drop 404 tons of bombs on the marshalling yards at Hameln and Holzmeinden. In addition, the bombers dropped 100 leaflet bombs on the inhabitants of Hagen, Herdecke, Hobenlemourne and Schwerte. One 'Window' aircraft was lost, but the rest came home – albeit with seven 323rd BG aircraft bearing scars from near misses by flak.

The following day some 334 medium bombers were despatched. Such a large force had the advantage of being able to attack targets which were fairly widely spread, although the 'primary' that day was the marshalling yard at Crailsheim. Supported by three 'Window' aircraft, the 323rd, 386th, 409th and 416th BGs destroyed the target at a cost of two aircraft lost and four with battle damage. One of the downed Marauders from the 323rd fell victim to an Me 262 attack, an eyewitness in another B-26 describing what happened;

'As we were on our way home and everything was going smoothly, I observed a twin-engined plane coming up behind the low flight – my first thought was that it was an A-26 lost from his group (and tagging onto us for security). The next thing I saw was smoke coming from one of our aircraft's tail guns. About this time, the right wingman went into a steep dive and disappeared through the clouds. With a jolt I realised that the "A-26" was an Me 262! By this time a second jet had scored a hit on the lead plane in the low flight, (and) he rolled over on his back and also disappeared through the clouds.'

Despite the Germans' plight, the last weeks of operations were nerve-wracking for the crews. Jets made everyone jumpy, and there were rumours that a desperate enemy was even resorting to using captured Allied aircraft to infiltrate bomber formations and cause carnage by suddenly opening fire. There was little truth in this, but the 'sightings' persisted – enough to keep trigger fingers 'itchy'. In such a tense atmosphere, a few friendly machines undoubtedly paid the price.

So many tactical targets had been destroyed that as the Allied pincers closed, bomber crews began feeling that they were being sent on sorties that did little more than maintain the momentum – the aerial equivalent of 'flogging a dead horse', with questionable military value. Such a mission took place on 20 April.

A maximum effort to bomb the

Barely had the shooting stopped when the 387th found itself on another base transfer, this time to Maastrich/Beek – or simply A-59 – in Belgium. There, a photographer captured part of a line up of Marauders in the 557th BS dispersal, including 42-107697 *Battlin'-Benny*, which completed 90 missions (*Crow*)

Venlo was the last wartime airfield used by the Marauders of the 397th BG, although their operations had actually finished by the time the unit moved in on 25 April 1945 – it went on to share the Dutch base with the 394th, who arrived the following month. There seems to have been some interchanging of aircraft at that time, as pilot Donald Elander of the 587th swears he flew this aircraft. With the shell case collector fitted, B-26G-25 44-67822 appears also to have been transferred in to the Ninth from one of the Twelfth AF groups, the overpainted vertical coloured band behind the tailplane being a giveaway – groups in the latter air force made extensive use of these as unit identifiers (*Crow*)

marshalling yards at Mimmingen would not, in the view of some participating crews from the 323rd, 394th and 397th BGs, achieve a great deal at that stage of the war. Sending every airworthy B-26 off was particularly annoying for those crews not scheduled to fly that day, as in some instances they were obliged to take the only available aircraft. Borrowed machines, sometimes from other squadrons in the group, were often considered to be 'suspect', as units would naturally offer their 'junk' in the form of 'near-hanger queens' that could barely stagger into the air. Such was the experience of 1Lt James Vining of the 455th BS/323rd BG, flying his 40th mission that day. What should have been a routine sortie was to prove to be more dramatic than anticipated.

At the controls of a 454th BS B-26F-1, Vining noted, with some irritation, that among the ship's myriad defects was a malfunctioning bomb release. Despite her 50-mission bomb log, 42-96256, nicknamed the *Ugly Duckling* by another pilot, was not exactly the best Marauder Vining had ever flown. Engine problems also delayed his take-off by some 30 minutes, but the group assembled in good order and crossed the Rhine west of Stuttgart on course for Memmingen, which lay to the south. Despite problems with his aircraft, Vining recalled that the morning brief had included an assurance that German aerial resistance had collapsed. There would be flak – but then again, when had there ever not been?

The formation droned on towards Memmingen. Flak bursts told crews they were nearing their objective, and approaching the IP at Kempten, the bomber boxes opened out so that single flights could release their loads in trail. Suddenly, they were being attacked by enemy aircraft – jets!

Behind the bombers, Unteroffizier Eduard Schallmoser of *Jagdverbande* 44 briefly tested his cannon, only to find that they would not fire. A jammed round had silenced his guns. This momentarily distracted the German pilot, who was closing fast on his quarry. Suddenly, an awful banging and tearing sound, accompanied by pieces of flying metal, told Schallmoser that he had been hit.

In fact, the Me 262 had been going too fast to pull up, and had flown through the propeller arc of the B-26 (44-68109) piloted by flight leader 1Lt James M Hansen. Both aircraft headed for the ground, the jet being followed by fire from the bomber gunners.

Schallmoser bailed out of his stricken fighter, but Hansen was able to fly his aircraft back to base. On impact with the B-26, the Me 262 had so uniformly bent back the propeller blades of the starboard engine that no noticeable vibration was transmitted through the shaft. The Twin Wasp continued to run as though nothing had happened.

While Schallmoser was unconventionally depleting one Marauder flight, James Vining's flight became the object of attention by other JV 44 aircraft. A flash of sunlight caught the jets as they swept in, cannon blazing. Vining thumbed the firing button and felt his quartet of package guns fire. Throughout the formation, pilots told their gunners to burn the barrels out of their weapons if necessary.

Eagerly the gunners responded to the surprise interception. Recalling the battle later, many men thought that the jets had not co-ordinated their attack very well, nor exploited their unquestioned performance edge. They also claimed that the barrage of fire from the massed 'fifties had scored a number of hits on the Me 262s, despite their great speed. Having to slow down to about the same speed as their piston-engined quarry in order to sight and fire with any accuracy was one of the major drawbacks the jet pilots faced. For a few precious seconds the bomber gunners had their chance, and a number of Me 262s were indeed damaged in this running fight with Marauders.

James Vining had troubles of his own. Wounded in the right foot by an exploding cannon shell that wrecked his control pedestal and probably severed the throttle linkage to the starboard engine (which promptly went to idle rpm), he called the co-pilot to take over. 1Lt James Mulvill instantly mastered the situation, and with direction from Vining, he brought the ship under control and nursed it in for a commendably steady crash-landing at Überherm – but for an unseen tank trap bordering the chosen field, he might have got away with it. The Marauder was totally wrecked in the ensuing crash, and it was later learned that the turret gunner, SSgt Charles Winger, had been killed.

Ignorant of the fact that it was JV 44 that attacked his formation that day, 1Lt Vining learned only years later that the jet unit crewed by the cream of the Luftwaffe's remaining *Experten* had been responsible. In total, the 323rd had lost three B-26s to the jets, whilst another aircraft had to be written off as a result of the damage it received and a further ten had to have holes patched.

On 24 April, the afternoon target for 74 B-26s of the 322nd and 344th BGs, plus 41 A-20s of the 410th, was a depot at Schrobenhausen, located about 30 miles north west of Munich. Alerted to this threat, Oberst Gunther Lutzow led five Me 262s of JV 44 to intercept south of Monheim. This they duly did, but the Marauders called in a P-47 escort, and although fire was exchanged, and a number of bombers damaged, the jets failed to shoot any of them down. It was during April that Generalleutnant Adolf Galland's Me 262 was damaged by return fire from B-26s of the 17th CBW. Also hit by P-47s, when Galland's battered Me 262 finally crash-landed, the wounds sustained by the CO of JV 44 in combat effectively put him out of the war – a considerable, albeit unrealised, coup for the B-26.

A plain aircraft from the 556th BS/387th BG, closely surrounded by other Marauders, shows that formation flying training was still being conducted in Germany as late as July 1945. A number of groups became part of the Occupation Forces, which was an unpopular move as men simply wanted to get home. Flying relieved the monotony for a lucky few, as many crews were indeed rotated back to the US within a few weeks of VE-Day. The serial number of B-26B-55 FW-B was 42-96189, this veteran bomber having previously seen service with the 344th BG (*Crow*)

More peaceful sightseeing, this time by a crew of the 494th BS/344th BG, photographed on a jaunt over Germany on 8 September 1945. The aircraft carries a fetching study of *Little Eve* on the nose and a simple black-outlined triangle on its tail. The wing walkway markings are quite prominent, perhaps denoting their fresh application (*Crow*)

Elsewhere, Marauders were being scrapped by the hundred. At Bad Worishopen, in Germany, they chopped up a number of B-26s assigned to the 397th and 322nd BGs, the latter's squadrons being fully represented in this grim shot by aircraft bearing the codes SS, ER, DR and PN. At left is B-26G-25 44-68163, late of the 451st BS. Down the right-hand line is an aircraft coded IH-X of the 1st Pathfinder Squadron (*Crow*)

Although it was the fighter fire which had inflicted the real damage, Galland had also previously been hit by the bomber gunners.

Interrogated after the war the ex-*General der Jagdflieger* stated the the B-26 was the one Allied aircraft he least liked to attack, even when flying an Me 262. He felt this was due both to the tight formations the Marauders flew and their heavy armament, which many German pilots were to grudgingly praise.

Hitting back at the Me 262s in the air was one way of whittling them down, but a far more effective method was to destroy them before they ever had the chance to take-off. Better still, the bombers could wreck them under construction, or in final assembly, so that only a trickle reached operational status. Before the end, Ninth BD flew many sorties to known jet aerodromes as soon as these were identified, whilst other raids were made on assembly points and vital POL (petroleum, oil and lubricants) production centres. The interdiction of Germany's rail system also achieved much, particularly as jet engines and parts had to be moved by this, the only economical method in terms of time.

On 25 April the 397th became the first of two Marauder groups to occupy the Dutch airfield at Venlo – the 394th moved there on 2 May. Venlo, alias Y-55 in the list of Allied codes for continental airfields, was a massive base, with some 32 miles of taxy strips lying partly inside Germany. Before abandoning it, the enemy had destroyed anything that might have been used by the Allied air forces, and therefore forced to live in in tents, the men of the 394th set about cleaning the place up. B-26s of the 1st Pathfinder Squadron also occupied Venlo, but no more operational sorties were flown.

Experience of jet fighter attacks on Marauders led to a sobering realisation that there was very little the units could do in the face of such opposition, but tight formations once again came into their own – 'close it up and put up curtains of .50 cal fire', best sums up the tactics used. This was hardly any different to the medium bombers' response to attack by any fighter, piston- or jet-powered, and it usually worked.

The basic station keeping devised for Marauder groups in 1943 still prevailed almost two years later, with two elements of three aircraft each forming a 'wing-over-wing' V. Each wingman (No 2 in the formation) flew very slightly above and behind his leader, and aligned the propeller hubs on the latter's top turret. No 4 acted as deputy lead, and flew slightly under and behind No 1, with Nos 5 and 6 on each wing. When flying these slots, the pilots lined up with the tail turret of the machine directly above them.

A tight pattern saved many a casualty when B-26s were attacked, American crews observing that their French comrades flying Marauders in the First Tactical Air Force let their formations become loose, thus allowing attacking fighters space enough to fly through them without having to turn away. That often resulted in crew casualties and damaged bombers.

The downside of good formation keeping was collision. This happened to one pilot when the B-26 immediately above him blew up. He could hardly avoid the debris, and was incredibly lucky to have escaped with nothing more serious than airframe damage to his Marauder. This was however, terminal, for when it landed, an examination showed that the main spar was damaged and the vertical control service were dangerously out of alignment. The Marauder never flew again.

Fighter escort for these late war missions also saved the B-26s from more losses, but crews could not always be certain exactly where the 'little friends' were. Escort was described variously as numbering from about 50 fighters (usually P-47s) 'close in', to 200 acting as 'area' escort. Bomber crews professed that they were never sure whether this meant that the fighters should be in their sight, or that they were above the clouds. 'Area' was taken to mean the target vicinity, but this again was vague.

Nevertheless, there were ostensibly so many Allied fighters up on clear days that help was never very far away, so medium bomber crews were not overly worried. However, a certain *laissez-faire* attitude appears to have pervaded briefings at that stage of the war because everyone knew the end could not be far off. Sadly, jet attacks showed that relaxing vigilance in any aspect of air operations over Germany was usually fatal. Fortunately for the Allies, the jet threat was never fully exploited by the enemy.

By late April only a few more sorties remained for the Ninth. By then, Marauder crews had honed medium altitude bombing to a fine art, as demonstrated by the 394th. In seven consecutive missions between the 17th and 20th against Magdeburg, oil installations at Wurzeburg and Nuremburg, and marshalling yards at Ulm and Memmingen, the 'Bridge Busters' achieved 'excellent' bombing results for the first four, and 'superior' for the last three. The group's final mission, flown on 20 April, was something of an anti-climax for its saw just six aircraft perform a leaflet drop – the group's 16th such operation of the war.

German stubbornness in resisting the inevitability of defeat led to the medium bombers attacking cities, which they only rarely done before. For example, the sorties against Magdeburg by the 394th's Marauders and the 386th's Invaders was designed to deter die-hard elements holding

Disposing of hundreds of unwanted Marauders in 1945 was a big job, and some were left to languish for many months. It was November before the wreckers got around to destroying *Patsy Ann*, an early model B-26B (probably a unit hack) of the 397th BG. That fate cannot have been far off when this photo was taken at Landsberg, the scene of so much postwar B-26 destruction (*H Holmes*)

Nose-art on a B-26G-20 of the 585th BS/394th BG. As can be seen in this, and other, photographs, the 394th did not make a regular practice of painting the pilot's name below the cockpit canopy (*Crow*)

out 'to the last man'. Medium bomber groups were each assigned a sector of the city, and widespread devastation would undoubtedly have resulted had Magdeburg not fallen to friendly troops.

A little closer to home for the Marauder men was the continual pounding of jet airfields, and locations such as Erding appeared to have special significance. Allied Intelligence had estimated that both this base and Freilassing ordnance depot were to be of major importance during last ditch Me 262 operations associated with Hitler's National Redoubt defence plan. The latter was, a myth but rumours persisted that die-hard Nazis would attempt to fortify and hold out in that area. The 'mediums' would attack both locations.

All six groups still flying the B-26 – the 322nd, 323rd, 344th, 387th, 394th and 397th – rounded out their individual combat records at much the same time, the mission to Erding aerodrome on 25 April being something of a Marauder 'swan song'. The B-26s of the 323rd and 344th, and Havocs of the 410th, made up a force of 296 aircraft which dropped 523 tons of bombs on the airfield.

As the formation approached Erding, the B-26 crews spotted a lone Me 262 coming at them from head-on. The strange jet was actually a test vehicle for the awesome Mk 214 cannon – a long range gun patterned after a tank weapon that fired a 50 mm shell that was designed to blast bombers out of the sky with a single round. Fortunately, it did not attack the B-26s, the gunners blazing away at it to deter the German pilot from chancing his luck. Although the strange-looking jet stayed out of range, the Marauder crews were shocked at the speed at which a Me 262 was able to reverse direction and approach from a different quadrant of sky in mere seconds. Other conventionally-armed Me 262s did open fire on the Marauders, however, but again the German pilots had to contend with the speed of their mounts being too high for effective, steady, attacks to be made. No bombers were lost.

Despite this distraction, the bombing was very accurate, with high explosive tearing up Erding's runway, and destroying eight aircraft and a number of buildings. The mission was the last for the white-tailed Marauders, as the 323rd was ordered to stand down the following day. Erding also turned out to be the last mission for the 344th, as a 'final final' mission the following day was recalled before the bombers reached the intended target – an aerodrome at Plattling.

On 3 May eight Pathfinder B-26s of the 1st PFS led Invaders of the 386th, 391st, 409th and 416th BGs over a European target (an ammunition dump at Stod) for the last time – there was virtually nothing left now for the 'mediums' to bomb. Six days later the Germans surrendered.

POST-MORTEM

Allied evaluation terms soon began combing Germany for tangible evidence of the giant strides in aeronautics that had been made before the end. Those achievements had made the B-26, and aircraft like it, obsolete, but that in no way detracted from the impressive force of arms the Ninth Air Force had represented. The medium bomber units made their last moves, with two groups, the 322nd and 323rd, going into Germany to Fritzlar (Y-86) and Gablingen (R-77) respectively, and the 387th to Maastricht/Beek (Y-44), in Holland. The rest remained at the Belgian

B-26G-10 of the 495th BS/394th BG showing some of the most striking artwork applied to Marauders in the ETO. This aircraft is depicted in the colour plates (*Crow*)

Another colour profile subject, *MISS MANOOKIE* of the 586th BS/394th BG had 50 missions recorded on its tally board. This particular play on words was very popular, and many combat aircraft besides B-26s adopted it (*Crow*)

and Dutch bases they had been flying from when hostilities ceased, and stayed put until such time as they were deactivated.

When peace came, the bald statistics of combat could not really do justice to the human cost of flying a B-26 Marauder over Europe, although the loss rate for all groups in the ETO was well inside established limits. Marauders had turned in one of the best combat records of any bomber, with sortie totals running into many thousands.

Heading the list of missions flown was, not surprisingly, the original quartet of Marauder groups that had joined the Eighth Air Force in 1943. 'Champion' was the 322nd, which had flown 428 missions, with the 323rd and 386th in joint second with an equal 409 each, followed by the 387th in third place, having chalked up 393. For the later groups, which made their combat debut in 1944, the 394th was typical with 271 missions, representing some 9036 sorties for the loss of 26 aircraft in action.

With occupation forces in place in Germany, the AAF quickly began a cull of those aircraft it no longer needed, quickly sealing the fate of the majority of B-26s. When the end came, it did so suddenly for many perfectly airworthy B-26s, with thousands being simply scrapped in Germany – blown up by explosive charge, the carcasses were disposed of by some of the same soldiers Ninth Air Force aircrews had been ordered to kill only weeks before. They, more than anyone, must have been mystified by the sudden turn of events, the swift and dramatic implementation of a 'swords into ploughshares' policy by their former enemies.

Virtually every A-20 in Germany was also scrapped, for along with the B-26, the Havoc was to be replaced by the A-26, this decision having been made more than a year before – therefore, this action seemed logical enough. Many war-weary P-51s were also broken up before the occupation forces were wound right down, the AAF having simply too many aircraft for envisaged peacetime requirements.

What rankled with Marauder veterans was the speed with which their B-26s were scrapped. It seemed to them that almost before the engines had cooled down from the last combat mission of the war, the bombers were sent off to collection points at places like Landsberg to be destroyed. It was as though somebody 'up there' could not be rid of Martin's 'medium' quickly enough. What really got their goat, however, was the fact that the Invader had the same identification number as the Marauder. This, they felt, was personal, particularly as postwar USAF aircraft designations dropped the attack category, and the Invader soon became the B-26. Ever since, veterans have been trying to explain to their nearest and dearest that they were Marauder, not Invader, crewmen in World War 2!

But such a harsh fate was not shared by all B-26s, and numerous examples could be seen in Germany during the first months of peace. The 344th, 394th and 397th BGs – the three youngest Marauder groups in the Ninth – became part of the occupation forces. Re-equipment with the Invader had not been completed by some groups before war's end, and the 394th, for example, operated B-26s while continuing conversion to the Douglas attack bomber. For other groups, abandoning their Marauders was but a step along the road to deactivation, and a ticket for the voyage home – a formal military movement almost universally welcomed.

No more positive a confirmation of the Marauder's prowess was

B-26B-55 42-96195 *Barbara Ann* was one of the bombing record holders in the 394th, completing some 135 mission – markers denoting these sorties were carefully stencilled below the cockpit (*Crow*)

needed than a glance at the lines of painted bombs representing combat missions which adorned so many of the Ninth Air Force veterans. All groups had had aircraft that accumulated 50 or more missions within a remarkably short period of them starting combat operations. Soon it became almost commonplace for groups to boast 100+ mission ships on their rolls. The second Marauder to reach this landmark after *MILD AND BITTER* was the 323rd's B-26C-10 41-34863, named *Bingo Buster*. *FLAK BAIT* was the third, then came B-26C-15 41-34951 *Impatient Virgin II* of the 322nd on 4 June 1944. By the end of July, the 322nd had another ten 100-mission Marauders – that same month six aircraft of the 386th made it as well. Other B-26s in this group soon followed, the 387th announcing its first five 'centenarians' during the summer. Such records would continue to be made.

As individual aircraft neared the 100-mission mark, crews (air and ground) began to worry for their safety. 'Lady Luck' surely had much to do with whether or not the century was achieved, and that fickle mistress did not always play the game by callously striking down a few contenders just short of the milestone. But an impressive number of 'centenarian' Marauders came through – as many as 350 of them (in all theatres) by war's end. The all-time B-26 mission record went to *FLAK BAIT* with no less than 202 sorties. It was more than fitting that the 322nd BG – the longest serving operational unit in the Eighth and Ninth Air Forces – was able to boast an aircraft with such an impressive record.

Most amazingly, despite all the 'brickbats' hurled at the B-26 during its short existence, the powers that be agreed to preserve *FLAK BAIT* when numerous other famous aircraft types took their combat record with them to the smelters. Even the 322nd's greatly-favoured *MILD AND BITTER* did not finally make it. A clear candidate for preservation, the aircraft was sent home to the States, along with *Bingo Buster*, in July 1944, but was subsequently destroyed in a crash.

Today, the scars visitors see on *FLAK BAIT*'s flanks when viewing it at the Smithsonian Institution's Air and Space Museum are real enough, and it is a no small irony that the one US aircraft to bear more genuine 'battle honours' than any other survivor of the mighty Army Air Forces in World War 2 should be a once much-maligned Martin Marauder!

Flak Bait **may not be the sole survivor of the 5157 Marauders built, but it is very nearly so, particularly following the unfortunate demise of the Confederate Air Force's flyable B-26C in September 1995. Although** *Flak Bait* **remains the most representative wartime survivor of the type, and as such is a prized exhibit in the Air and Space Museum in Washington, D C, Marauder veterans and warbird enthusiasts alike are currently working towards the day when another B-26 regularly takes to the skies in the USA (***H Holmes***)**

APPENDICES

MARAUDER UNITS OF THE NINTH

Movement of B-26 groups between 1943 and 1945. Dates for UK bases generally relate to the first mission flown, whilst continental base dates are from arrival.

322nd Bomb Group

Andrews Field	12 June 1943
Beuvais/Tille (France)	25 September 1944
Le Culot (France)	30 March 1945

323rd Bomb Group

Earls Colne	16 July 1943
Beaulieu	18 July 1944
Kessay (France)	26 August 1944
Chartres (France)	21 September 1944
Laon/Athies (France)	13 October 1944
Denain/Prouvy (France)	9 February 1945

344th Bomb Group

Stansted	29 February 1944
Cormeilles-en-Vexin (France)	30 September 1944
Florrenes/Juzains (Belgium)	5 April 1945

386th Bomb Group

Boxted	30 July 1943
Great Dunmow	24 September 1943
Beaumont-sur-Oise (France)	2 October 1944
St Trond (Belgium)	9 April 1945

387th Bomb Group

Chipping Ongar	15 August 1943
Stoney Cross	23 July 1944
Maupertus (France)	1 September 1944
Chateaudun (France)	18 September 1944
Clasters (France)	4 November 1944

391st Bomb Group

Matching	15 February 1944
Roye/Amy (France)	19 September 1944
Asch (Belgium)	20 April 1945

394th Bomb Group

Boreham	23 March 1944
Holmsley South	24 July 1944
Tour-en-Bessin (France)	20 July 1944
Cambrai/ Niergnies (France)	8 October 1944
Venlo (Holland)	2 May 1945

397th Bomb Group

Gosfield	No missions flown
Rivenhall	20 April 1944
Hurn	5 August 1944
Gorges (France)	30 August 1944
Dreux (France)	15 September 1944
Péronne (France)	7 October 1944
Venlo (Holland)	25 April 1944

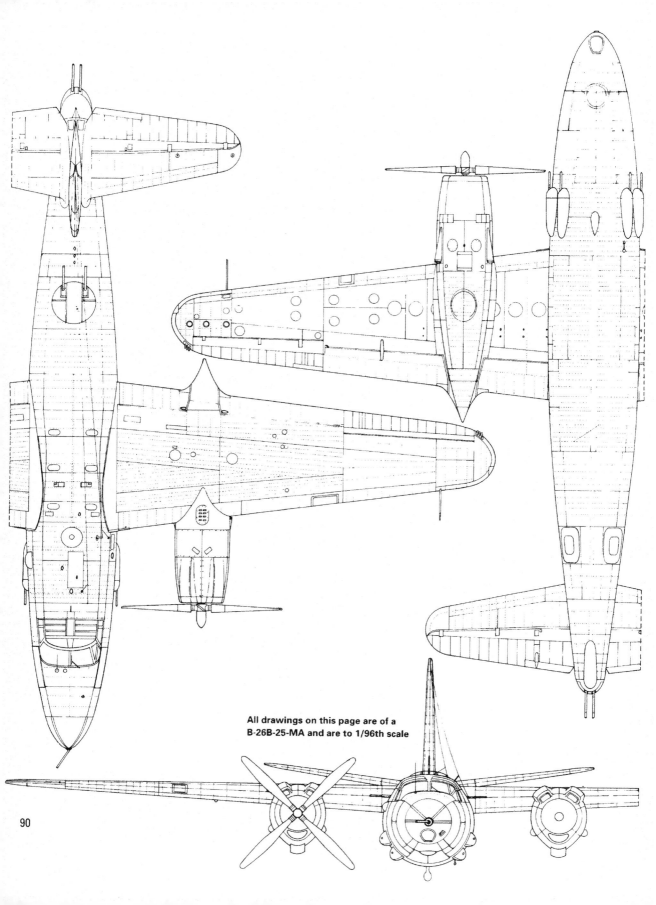

All drawings on this page are of a
B-26B-25-MA and are to 1/96th scale

90

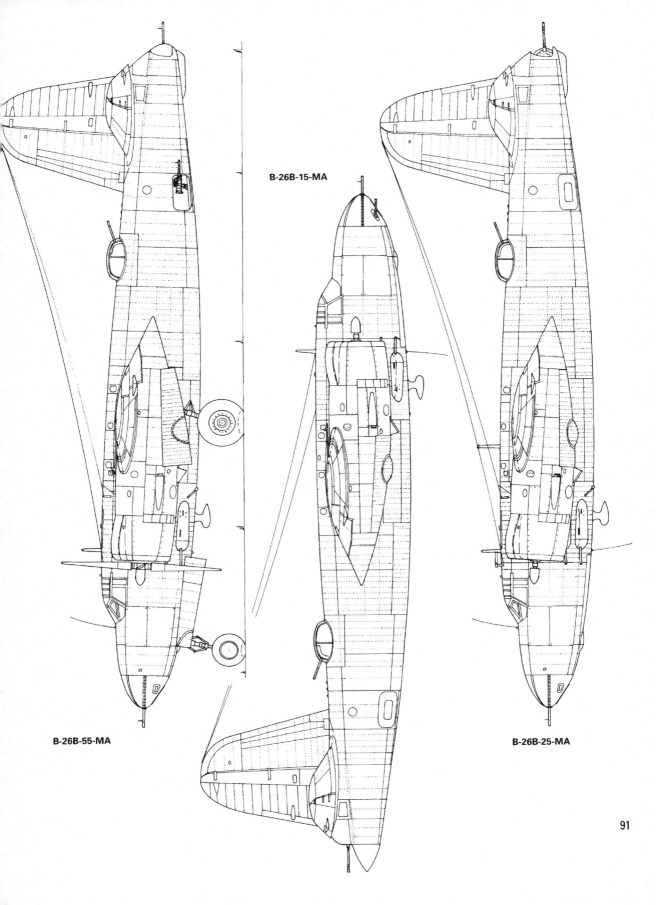

B-26B-15-MA

B-26B-55-MA

B-26B-25-MA

COLOUR PLATES

1

B-26B-10-MA 41-18272/PN-Q *MURDER INC* of the 449th BS/322nd BG

The American penchant for naming combat aircraft was quickly adopted on ETO B-26s, this example probably owing its sobriquet more to the Edward G Robinson gangster film of the same name, rather than any darker intent. The three-tone finish has been credited with originating in the MTO as a 'Mediterranean patrol' scheme, and was probably also influenced by Stateside sea-search paint experiments with B-26s. Fin de-icer boots were short-lived.

2

B-26B-25-MA 41-31814/ER-F *Bag of Bolts* of the 450th BS/322nd BG

Having the widely-applied, but short-lived, red outline to its US national insignia as depicted in September 1943, this B-26 is believed to have carried its name on the port side of the nose only. One of the unfortunate aircraft that just missed its century, 41-31814 went MIA on the night of 7/8 July 1944 whilst on its 98th mission. The 322nd lost no less than nine B-26s on that night.

3

B-26G-5-MA 43-34409/SS-M of the 451st BS/322nd BG

This aircraft is believed to be one of the 322nd's 'anonymous' Marauders (not all USAAF combat aircraft were named), although it may have borne some personalised marking on the port side – traditionally the most favoured, simply because that was the side the pilot sat on. A similar application of top surface camouflage was seen on other natural metal finish (NMF) aircraft within this unit.

4

B-26B-4-MA 41-17995/DR-T *TONDELAYO* of the 452nd BS/322nd BG

Col Robert Stillman flew this aircraft when he acted as deputy lead to Capt Roland Scott, formation leader on the first Imjuiden raid on 14 May 1943. It was not selected to fly the second, and by missing this debacle, and surviving a subsequent 'hairy' incident, the new name of *Mr Period Twice* seemed appropriate! The aircraft flew some 20 sorties

before the 322nd converted to 'big wing' Marauders, whereupon it was probably retired to second line duties.

5

B-26C-6-MO 41-34727/VT-O *TICKELISH PERCY* of the 453rd BS/323rd BG

One of the original aircraft brought to England by 'The Crusaders', this machine (and a number of others like it) had the two small observation windows above the waist hatch, which were soon deleted. Relatively new items such as the package guns were obscured by wartime censors in photographs released to the press. The aircraft is depicted in the summer of 1943, the red outlined-insignia being officially introduced on 29 June.

6

B-26C-45-MO 41-2107582/RJ-B of the 454th BS/323rd BG

Although this Marauder apparently had no name, it more than made up for it through the application of a rare shark's mouth – only a handful of B-26s (in the Ninth at least) had such nose-art applied to them. This aircraft is depicted in profile as its appeared in early 1944, having completed three missions. Removing camouflage from the vertical tail surfaces of its Marauders, even when fuselage paintwork was retained, was common practice in the 323rd. This necessitated outlining the tail band in black.

7

B-26C-15-MO 41-34955/YU-T *MISSION BELLE* of the 455th BS/323rd BG

One of the group's 'centenarian' Marauders, the '*Belle* was the second in the group to achieve this feat, *Bingo Buster* having been the first. Suitably battle-stained, the aircraft has the red outline to its upper wing insignia overpainted in dark blue, although the fuselage markings has been completely re-done.

8

B-26B-20-MA 41-31722/WT-A *Smokey* of the 456th BS/323rd BG

With a typically battered and scarred olive drab finish, this machine shows evidence of having 'borrowed' some sections from sister-ships to keep it flying. Flak damage was extensive on many B-26s in the ETO, and metal patching inevitably led to worn and faded paintwork. Paint removal, when it was carried out, instantly improved the look of some aircraft.

9

B-26G-5-MA 43-34384/K9-B *Little EVE* of the 494th BS/344th BG

A late-war delivery to the squadron, this aircraft may not have had time to fly too many combat missions, but it did survive to undertake a number of training sorties in the immediate aftermath of war as part of the occupation forces, which remained in Germany for some months. Although the bomber is shown with a white centre to the triangle marking, it also flew a number of sorties with just a black outline to the group identifier.

10

B-26C-45-MO 41-2107666/Y5-F *BARRACUDA* of the 495th BS/344th BG

Never quite matching the ferocious look captured by Marauders of the 444th BS in the MTO, individual Ninth Air Force B-26s were nevertheless marked up in a similar fashion by crews who wanted their aircraft to stand out on a packed flightline. This aircraft has 42 missions symbols on its tally board, and is depicted as it looked in late 1944.

11

B-26B-50-MA 42-95870/N3-B *MAXWELL HOUSE - GOOD TO THE LAST DROP* of the 496th BS/344th BG

The commercial rider 'Good to the last drop' was tailor-made for a tactical bomber – and to distinguish the personal aircraft of Capt Jewel Maxwell, CO of 496th BS. This was his second 'named' B-26, the first having been lost whilst being flown by another crew in April 1944.

12

B-26B-50-MA 42-95902/7I-G of the 497th BS/344th BG

Another variation in treatment of camouflage, this aircraft retains the medium green 'splotched' finish designed to break up its outline in the event of attack by enemy interceptors. It was totally ineffective against flak, however, the B-26's main adversary in the ETO.

13

B-26B-15-MA 41-31617/RG-A *Winnie* of the 552nd BS/386th BG

Usually flown by Maj Charles W 'Chuck' Lockhart, 552nd BS CO, this aircraft had the squadron insignia (a winged skull and bomb on a yellow background) painted on the nosewheel cover. The name *Winnie* appeared on both sides of the nose, together with a mission log which began modestly enough (like many Eighth Air Force Marauders) with a couple of decoy ducks, denoting diversionary raids.

14

B-26G-1-MA 43-34210/AN-V *LA PALOMA* of the 553rd BS/386th BG

One of many B-26s that had its name applied to both sides of the nose, but with no discernible bomb log – the application of such mission markings were, of course, left to the discretion of the individual crew. The aircraft is depicted as it appeared at the group's austere base at Beaumont-sur-Oise, in France, during the harsh winter of 1944-45.

15

B-26B-25-MA 41-31832/RU-U of the 554th BS/386th BG

Shown as it appeared at Great Dunmow, Essex, in the late summer of 1944, this aircraft had a more or less 'regulation' olive drab and grey finish, and is believed to have been devoid of any personal markings – at least on the starboard side. The 386th flew numerous Marauders in standard finish through to the end of their service, which was curtailed by the arrival of A-26 Invaders in late 1944, followed by the commencement of combat operations in February 1945.

16

B-26B-55-MA 42-96131/YA-P *Perkatory II* of the 555th BS/386th BG

This aircraft was in effect a replacement for Bob Perkins *Perkatory*, which was destroyed when a Ju 88 crashed onto it after being shot down by an RAF Mosquito during a night raid on Earls Colne in March 1944. Stripped back to natural metal finish in time to fly invasion support sorties, it appears not to have received any upper surface camouflage, this becoming increasingly superfluous as the war progressed.

17

B-26B-50-MA 42-95857/FW-K *Shootin in* of the 556th BS/387th BG

A replacement for another 556th BS Marauder, this aircraft took its name from an expression frequently used by the co-pilot on 1Lt Asa V Clark's crew when they took it over. Lt Ben Van-Cleave became skipper while the group was based at Chateaudun, and '857 was also flown by a Lt Patterson, who was at the controls on 19 April 1945 when the bomber completed its 135th, and last, mission.

18

B-26C-45-MO 42-107697/KS-P *BATTLIN'-BENNY* of the 557th BS/387th BG

Regulations to ensure that unit code letters and serial numbers remained readable when invasion stripes and tactical camouflage were applied were fairly broadly interpreted at group level. This machine went on to fly a further 90 missions following its combat debut over the D-Day beaches on 6 June 1944 – its regular pilot was a Lt Dempster.

19

B-26B-55-MA 42-96205/KX-N *HAMILTON "HEY" MAKER II* of the 558th BS/387th BG

When this B-26 was passed onto the 387th's 558th BS by the 397th BG, its new crew retained the cowgirl nose-art applied by the latter unit – the 387th's tail band was also painted on straight over the diagonal stripe marking of its former owners. Removal of old tail markings was deemed to be unimportant at the end of the war.

20

B-26B-30-MA 41-31874/TQ-Q *BOOGER RED II* of the 559th BS/387th BG

Piloted for much of its career by the appropriately named Lt Jack Skipper, this aircraft was damaged during 'ultra low' flying training before the group became operational. Once repaired, it went on to fly more than 100 missions, and was later flown by 1Lt John Sivert. On 15 August 1944 he scored a direct hit on a bridge with two 2000-lb bombs whilst flying this very machine. Badly shot up during a massive fighter attack on 23 December, '874 somehow made it back to base but never flew again.

21

B-26-B-45-MA 42-95816/P2-S of the 572nd BS/391st BG

The aircraft of some Ninth Air Force Marauder units seemed to be more rarely photographed than others, and the 391st BG, nicknamed 'The Black Death Group' by its CO, Col Gerald Williams, was a perfect case in point. The handful of contemporary images available show that aircraft of this squadron retained standard camouflage for quite some time.

22

B-26C-45-MO 42-107740/T6-U *Junior* of the 573rd BS/391st BG

This Marauder came home from a sortie so severely battle damaged that official photographs were taken at its Matching, Essex, base upon its return. The damage had been caused on 20 May 1944 when an 88 mm flak shell sliced off the top of the fin and rudder, and stripped most of the skin off the elevators – it was nevertheless restored to its former glory by a Mobile Repair and Reclamation Squadron and went on the fly a total of 96 missions. Throughout its long combat career, '740 remained a 'plain' B-26, with only its upper nose and inner-facing engine nacelles being painted in olive drab.

23

B-26B-50-MA 42-95840/4L-R *SAM CRAM!* of the 574th BS/391st BG

Another B-26 that retained the medium green mottle over olive drab finish for quite some time after the latter shade had been exclusively chosen for upper surface application, it is not known if '*SAM* later went on to have its finish modified. It was common for individual aircraft to keep the same camouflage and detail markings throughout their frontline service careers – sometimes through to VE-Day, if they survived on operations for that long.

24

B-26B-45-MA 42-95808/O8-C *Idiot's Delight* of the 575th BS/391st BG

Depicted before its AEAF black and white 'invasion' stripes were applied, '808 is seen very much the worse for wear. Due to the arduous schedule of missions performed in the lead up to D-Day, the drab finish on many B-26s often failed to 'stay the distance', peeling away in great swathes to the point where the aircraft often looked to be in far worse physical shape than was really the case. Underneath all the scratches, the medium green mottle remained visible on the wings, vertical tail and horizontal stabiliser surfaces.

25
B-26G-10-MA 43-34571/K5-Y ROUND TOO! of the 584th BS/394th BG

A 'clean' Marauder without any embellishment, apart from the nose-art (in this instance a well executed 'original' by artist Frank Spangler) on the armour plate panel, this aircraft had no bomb log applied when photographed at the 394th BG's base at Cambrai, in France, in early 1945.

26
B-26G-1-MA 43-34213/4T-C THE OLD GOAT of the 585th BS/394th BG

Allowing the upper surface tactical camouflage to run behind the code letters made the latter hard to read from any distance, but by the end of the war it was deemed not to matter too much. This aircraft was also based at A-74, or Cambrai, in early 1945.

27
B-26F-1-MA 42-96255/H9-P MISS MANOOKIE of the 586th BS/394th BG

Again wearing a rendering by the prolific artist Frank Spangler, this aircraft bears a nickname that appeared on Allied bombers in all the major theatres of World War 2. Spangler was one of a number of talented artists whose work was much sought after by flight crews, and although having to paint directly onto metal surfaces, this appeared to present him with few problems. This Marauder was one of 100 B-26F-1 models built, and it completed more than 60 missions.

28
B-26F-1-MA 42-96281/5W-V Redlight Rosie of the 587th BS/394th BG

A 394th BG 'centenarian', this aircraft flew a total of 107 missions between its first, on 13 June 1944, and VE-Day. It is shown as it appeared at Cambrai in late 1944, its pilot at the time being a Lt J V Roy.

29
B-26B-55-MA 42-96153/X2-N of the 596th BS/397th BG

Christened The Joker, this aircraft had both nose-art and named engines, as well as a striking red 'cheatline' that ran the length of the fuselage and red flashes on the engine cowlings. Like a number of other Marauders in the Ninth Air Force, this machine appears not to have had its nickname actually painted on it – '153 had actually borne another name when assigned to an earlier crew within the group.

30
B-26B-55-MA 42-96191/9F-N THE MILK RUN SPECIAL of the 597th BS/397th BG

An example of the high standard of artwork achieved by some groundcrew painters, the 'SPECIAL had flown 43 missions by the time it was photographed wearing the markings shown here, her regular crew at that time being led by a Lt Overbey. The aircraft completed more than 100 sorties, and although the 397th was based at Péronne, in France, at war's end, it was photographed visiting Steeple Morden, home of the 355th FG, in the spring of 1945.

31
B-26B-55-MA 42-96138/U2-C By-Golly of the 598th BS/397th BG

Flown by Capt John Quinn West, a man with unshakeable religious principles, this aircraft was named after the strongest language he would ever stoop to! It is depicted here as it looked following the completion of its 26th mission soon after D-Day. It survived until 16 July 1944, when it was destroyed in a crash landing at A-7 (Azeville). West was awarded a DFC for his skill in bringing the damaged B-26 down, but was himself killed on 1 August when his replacement aircraft was shot down by German fighters.

32
B-26B-55-MA 42-96165/6B-T of the 599th BS/397th BG

Another B-26 that was apparently widely known within the 599th BS by its nickname – in this case, 'The Big Hairy Bird' – yet did not appear to have had this actual nickname applied, '165 was easily the most strikingly decorated Marauder to see action in any theatre. Flown by a pilot named Shaeffer whilst part of the 397th, it was eventually passed to the 387th BG shortly before war's end, the latter group simply applying its black and yellow horizontal tail stripe in place of the yellow diagonal band as seen here.

33
B-26G-1-MA 43-34195/Yellow X of the 654th BS/25th BG, Eighth Air Force

One of four B-26Gs operated by the 25th BG on

Dilly missions to photograph V1 sites at night during July 1944, this was the third machine converted to recce configuration at Mount Farm, where cameras were installed and extraneous equipment removed to improve the aircraft's performance. It flew just three sorties in this role as the 'flying bomb' sites were soon overrun. However, the Marauder was retained by the 25th for training and other second line duties until March 1945.

34

B-26B-50-MA 42-95867/IH-A1 of the 1st Pathfinder Squadron (Provisional)

Originally formed from a nucleus of veteran 322nd BG crews who were retrained for the exacting pathfinder role using 'Oboe', this aircraft is one of the few definitely recorded as having belonged to the unit. The unusual code and double individual aircraft letter combination possibly indicated that there were two aircraft coded A on the squadron's strength – other Marauders within this elite unit had conventional codes.

FIGURE PLATES

1

Lt Ralph N Phillips of the 455th BS/323rd BG was the first B-26 crewman (navigator) to complete 50 ETO missions, and he is seen here in an M1 steel helmet that has been personalised with a 'flying eight ball' badge and bomb markers, the latter complete with mission details. Aircrew injuries were greatly reduced by the arrival of the M1 flak vest with M3 apron, which is shown here worn over an A2 leather jacket with rank badges attached to the shoulder straps. Officers' pattern trousers (known as 'pinks') and russet brown shoes complete the uniform.

2

Capt Hugh Fletcher, bombardier with the 452nd BS/322nd BG, is depicted wearing an A9 summer flying helmet, A2 jacket, dark brown officers' pattern trousers and russet brown shoes. The A4 QAC parachute harness, with chest 'chute detached, is worn over a B4 life vest. Fletcher's Jack Russell terrier 'Salvo' had a custom-made harness complete with miniature 'chute, which he used on numerous descents. 'Salvo' would bale out with Fletcher during training flights designed to test ease of crew exit from stricken B-26s.

3

SSgt 'Denny' McFarland of the 553rd BS/386th BG served as tail gunner in 164-mission B-26B *Rat Poison*. He is seen here wearing standard issue 1944 US Army Air Forces NCO's head wear, which comprised an overseas cap with branch of service piping and insignia. His khaki field jacket is adorned with badges of rank and a Ninth AF patch. The uniform is completed by matching olive drab shirt and trousers, a khaki tie and russet brown boots.

4

Col Jack Caldwell, CO of the 387th BG, is seen clothed in a representative aircrew uniform as worn by UK-based medium bombardment groups in the spring of 1944. He has a HS 38 headset with officers' pattern garrison cap and rank badge, an A4 QAC parachute harness (chest type, shown without a 'chute) over a B.3 life preserver vest, A2 jacket and an A4 summer flying suit. Gloves are of the A-11 type, and note the knife strapped to his life preserver harness – his shoes are of the A-6 winter type. Caldwell, who did much to develop Ninth BC's medium level attack techniques, was killed in action in April 1944 soon after his personal Marauder, *The Arkansas Traveller*, had been lost whilst being flown by another crew.

5

Capt Louis Sebille served as a pilot with the 450th BS/322nd BG, and is depicted wearing a standard officers' visor service cap, with stiffeners in place, and matching dark brown shirt and trousers, which was again regulation issue for US Army officers. Captain's bars are attached to the right collar, with USAAF insignia on the left, whilst embroided bullion and pilots' wings appear on the left breast of his shirt. Note Sebille's civilian pattern belt. The Marauder veteran was later awarded a posthumous Medal of Honor after being killed in action flying a F-51 Mustang in Korea in August 1950.

6

Capt Norman Harvey flew with the 449th BS/322nd BG, and is seen wearing an M1 steel helmet and an A9 flying helmet, fitted with B-7 goggles and a throat microphone. An M1 aircrew flak vest with M3 apron are worn over a life preserver and an S1 seat-type parachute harness. An A2 flying jacket and A4 summer flying suit, plus A11 gloves and russet brown field 'shoes', complete the picture.

INDEX

References to illustrations are shown in **bold**. Colour Plates (cp.) and Figure Plates (fp.) are shown with page and caption locators in brackets.